QUARTET

THE FRE

This remarkable journal of experiences and ideas, set down during the period 1912–13 by the novelist, poet, essayist and 'emancipated woman', warmly records her studies with Freud and his pupils at a particularly dramatic time in the life of psychoanalysis. Taking the reader into Freud's inner world through her many personal reflections on him and his relations with his colleagues and students, the *Journal* offers fresh insights into an age and many of its principal writers – Rilke among them.

LOU ANDREAS-SALOME

Lou Andreas-Salomé was born in St Petersburg in 1861. Her extraordinary life encompassed a great variety of famous people and momentous events. A novelist and critic, she was also a keen disciple of Freud. Her relations with great men undoubtedly contributed to her reputation, but her aura of superiority was one which many people found entirely justified. Freud paid many tributes to her; Nietzsche said of her: 'I have never known a more gifted or more understanding creature'; Rilke wrote of her: 'She moves fearlessly midst the most burning mysteries . . .' She died in 1937.

LOU ANDREAS-SALOME

The Freud Journal

Translated from the German by
STANLEY A. LEAVY
With an Introduction by
MARY-KAY WILMERS

QUARTET ENCOUNTERS

Quartet Books   London   New York

Published by Quartet Books Limited 1987
A member of the Namara Group
27/29 Goodge Street, London W1P 1FD

British Library Cataloguing in Publication Data

Andreas-Salomé, Lou
  The Freud journal.
  1. Freud, Sigmund   2. Psychoanalysis
  I. Title
  150.19'52   BF173.F85

  ISBN 0-7043-0022-2

Reproduced, printed and bound in Great Britain
by The Camelot Press plc, Southampton

CONTENTS

Preface

Acknowledgments for assistance in preparing my translation of "In der Schule bei Freud" (Zürich: Max Niehans Verlag, 1958) are especially due to three persons: First to the editor of the German text, Herr Ernst Pfeiffer of Göttingen, whose reading has been used as it was originally published by him and whose explanatory notes I have freely consulted. Second, I wish to express my thanks to Mrs. Eva Kessler of New Haven, who has very carefully read the text and in innumerable places has suggested a more graceful or more faithful translation. Third, I am indebted to Prof. Rudolph Binion of Columbia University, who in many letters and conversations has shared with me his knowledge of the life, work, and character of Lou Andreas-Salomé.

I have found Dr. H. F. Peters' recent biography, "My Sister, My Spouse" (New York: W. W. Norton, 1962), very helpful; it also contains an excellent bibliography of the writings of Lou-Andreas-Salomé. Miss Anna Freud kindly related to me some of her personal recollections of her and her father's friend. Mrs. Lottie M. Newman and Dr. Hans W. Loewald have made valuable suggestions. I am grateful to Prof. Albert Ehrenzweig of the University of California, Berkeley, for his translation of the poem "Narziss" by Rainer M. Rilke.

Mrs. Grete Heinemann expertly prepared the final manuscript. To my wife I am obligated for her interest and her patience in the long presence of this invisible but formidable guest.

STANLEY A. LEAVY

INTRODUCTION

Lou Andreas-Salomé was in her time one of the most admired women in Central Europe; and among women with a claim to intellectual achievement probably the most famous. In September 1911, at the height of her renown, she attended the Third Psychoanalytic Congress in Weimar. Freud, who didn't believe there was much in psychoanalysis that could be understood by an outsider, was nonetheless flattered to see her there. A year later, she arrived in Vienna to study psychoanalysis at first hand: 'the sole aim of my visit,' she had written to Freud, 'is to devote myself further to every aspect of this matter.' Freud was quite evidently pleased. That such a distinguished Gentile should be taking a serious interest in what he and his colleagues were thinking augured well for the respectability of the movement. Besides, she had a compelling personality and, it soon became clear, an unusual capacity to understand other people's ideas. Freud's colleague Karl Abraham, who got to know her a few months before Freud did, had been bowled over: 'I have never,' he said, 'met anyone with so deep and subtle an understanding of psychoanalysis.'

When she came to Vienna in October 1912, she had read everything Freud had written. She left in April the following year and *The Freud Journal* is largely a record of those six months. In it she noted, not so much the things that she did, as what was said at the lectures and meetings she attended, the ideas that other people had and those they quarrelled over, and her own thoughts about all this. She was then fifty-one. She had published several novels and other books, among them studies of Nietzsche and Ibsen, as well as essays on the three subjects that were always closest to her heart – religion, love and the psychology of women. She was living in

Göttingen, but spent several months each year travelling to the centres of European cultural life, seeking out important people, involving herself, with the enthusiasm which characterized everything she did, in whatever artistic or intellectual enterprise they were currently engaged in, and earnestly discussing their ideas with them – a section at the end of *The Freud Journal*, for example, reports a 'fine' conversation with the philosopher Max Scheler on the Greek theory of motion. Wherever she went she was marvelled at. Only Tolstoy failed to be impressed. The first time she met him he was more interested in her husband. On the second occasion, when she and Rilke travelled to Yasnaya Polyana to see him, he was busy quarrelling with his wife and told them they could choose between lunch 'with the others' and a walk round the garden with him.

Born Louise von Salomé in St Petersburg in 1861, the youngest child and only daughter of a former general in the Tsar's army, she'd been married since 1887 to Friedrich Carl Andreas, a professor of Western Asiatic Languages in the University of Göttingen. The marriage, like all her relationships with men, was conducted rather more obviously for her benefit than for his. Before she married she had had a considerable number of celebrated suitors, but though she liked to be admired, and to admire, she wasn't interested in the usual relationships that women have with men, at least not then: when these suitors proposed either marriage or an affair, she turned them down. By far the most celebrated of her celebrated admirers was Nietzsche and it's evident that she was far more successful than he was in leading the life of a Nietzschean free spirit.

After her marriage she had a succession of sexual relationships with men who were much younger than she was. When the relationship had outlived whatever purpose, direct or indirect, it had originally served, she brought it to an end. It's also thought by some that she had affairs with women but although this isn't entirely unlikely, the evidence is obscure. One way or another, however, she never did what she might have been expected to do. She never, for instance, slept with her husband: he had a child by the maid. One of the incidental pleasures of this journal are the passages where she expounds her ideas on the sexual nature of women and explains, in a lofty tone of voice, as if none of it had anything to do with her, why it was to the general advantage of everyone for women to disregard moral convention. She was a strikingly handsome and intelligent woman; and she had a ruthless sense of her own destiny. There is nonetheless some irony in the fact that what brought her her fame was the intensity of her relationships with men who were even more famous than she was. She had, as Ernest Jones put it in his biography of Freud, 'a remarkable flair for great men'.

The first, and the greatest, of these was God. 'My earliest memory,' she said more than once, 'is of my acquaintance with God.' This wasn't, however, the usual God who is communally worshipped in church and loves all his flock equally: her God existed 'wholly for me alone', and no one else knew about him. When one day he failed to answer her call she ceased to believe in him, but characteristically turned disappointment to advantage, eventually deciding that God had been created by man's need to believe in him, that this need was a mark of human greatness, and that what mattered was religious feeling – not religion. Necessarily vague, it was a comforting solution to nineteenth-century doubts about the existence of God. These ideas stayed with her all her life and reappear in different guises in everything she wrote, including this journal, where there is much cloudy talk, less obviously Freudian than Jungian, of 'grand totalities' and of the union of the self with something larger, which is sometimes an undefined 'beyond' and at others is spoken of as a mysterious a-historical collective called 'the entire past of mankind'.

Freud, though he seems always to have considered her a wholly superior being and, according to Ernest Jones, thought especially well of her 'ethical ideals, which he felt far transcended his own', was never very taken with this kind of abstract speculation. Their differences, perhaps not surprisingly given Lou's sense of herself, were focused on the self-loving figure of Narcissus. Freud, already in 1912 engaged in writing the essay on narcissism which was published two years later, was concerned to work out the dynamics of a pathological state of mind which he took Narcissus to epitomize. For Lou, on the other hand, Narcissus was always a hero, whose self-love – in itself no defect – was so great that it could only be fulfilled by merging with the 'boundless world of nature' as represented by the pool in which he drowned, heroically gazing at his own reflection.

God's immediate successor in Lou's life was one of his pastors, Hendrik Gillot, the 'most brilliant' Protestant preacher in St Petersburg. She was then seventeen and had chosen Gillot to prepare her for her Confirmation in preference to the more humdrum family pastor. For her it was the beginning of an outstanding career as prophet's disciple. Or teacher's pet. Unfortunately, after a time desire got the better of Gillot, and he proposed to her. Lou was appalled, fell ill and, when she was better, left the country. After a year in Zurich, where she was one of the first women to study at the university, her mother took her to Rome.

It was there that she met, first, Paul Rée, author of *The Origin of Moral Feelings*, and then his friend Nietzsche. Each in turn was eager to marry her – Nietzsche was sure he had found his *alter ego*. She turned them down but hoped that she might even so set up house with the two of them and with them lead the life of conversation and intellectual inquiry which, before her marriage, was all she wanted of men. The more accommodating Rée was happy to go along with this, and for three years he and Lou lived chastely together, defying both bourgeois and bohemian expectations. Nietzsche, however, not quite the *supermensch*, after six months of hectic enthusiasm ('I wonder if there has ever existed before such a philosophical openness as exists between us'), yielded to his sister's poisonous jealousy of Lou, and fearing the break-up of his family, refused to see her again. Once he had spoken of their 'intelligence and tastes' being 'related at the deepest point': now she was a 'dry, dirty, nasty-smelling monkey with false breasts'. The association with Nietzsche nonetheless brought her substantial benefits, intellectually and in the eyes of the world – from then on there were few people who weren't flattered to be the object of her attention. Nietzsche also gave her the confidence – or maybe only the excuse – to live her life exactly as she wanted to live it. 'I have never actually known the feeling of choice,' she wrote in her diary for 1882, 'but found in myself much analogy with the necessary working of natural forces.' Nietzsche was never as sublimely convinced that he should have what he wanted – at least not in his day-to-day life.

It isn't clear why the next thing she wanted was to marry Andreas: but it was, and in so doing she lost Rée for good. Nor is it clear why a marriage which, at her insistence, was never consummated should in some sense have acted as a sexual inspiration. It was in 1897 that she met Rilke, her first lover, but five years before that she'd been on the verge of running off with a charismatic left-wing journalist. Neither *The Freud Journal* nor her autobiography has anything to say about all this. Her interest in psychoanalysis, she explains in the journal, was largely a consequence of her concern for Rilke and his precarious state of mind. There is no evidence here or elsewhere that she saw any reason to apply the insights of psychoanalysis to her own life or behaviour; and although she admired Freud for what she saw as his heroic endeavour to understand himself, when she wrote about her own life it was always in terms of the entire female gender. 'Should we not be moved,' she says about Freud, 'by the knowledge that he might have attained his greatness only through his frailties?' The fact that she herself wasn't conscious of having any frailties makes one wonder how she knew.

Rilke was twenty-one when she met him. She herself was in her late thirties and there was undoubtedly a strong maternal element in their relationship. Gillot and Nietzsche had been her mentors; Rilke, while being her lover, was also her pupil, though it's hard to believe that she would have given him so much time had she not had a powerful sense of his talent. But he was also more neurotically dependent than she could bear and after three years she was desperate to be rid of him: 'To make Rainer go, go right away,' she noted in her diary in January 1901, 'I would be capable of real brutality.' In the event she was quite brutal but for the rest of his life she continued to look after him when he needed her – to act, even before her engagement with psychoanalysis, as his therapist; and though some commentators have not liked the effect that their relationship had on him, it seems possible that he would have sunk into a morbid silence had it not been for her insistence that he re-route what sometimes threatened to be an incapacitating preoccupation with himself into his work.

She was in general a level-headed woman, as she perhaps needed to be if she was going to get her own way as often as she did. Having arrived in Vienna with every advantage reputation can bring, she immediately set about making herself Freud's favourite person. She had only been there two weeks when she missed one of his lectures: 'I stared as if spellbound at the vacant chair reserved for you,' he told her later. He wrote her 'sweet' letters, sent her flowers, invited her to his house, walked her home late at night. He, too, needed her. 1912 marked the beginning of a sequence of rifts between Freud and, on the one hand, those of his colleagues who disagreed with him, like Adler, Stekel and Jung, and on the other, those who he feared might be trying to get to his ideas before he did. Of these Viktor Tausk was at that time the most prominent. A good-looking, troubled man, eighteen years younger than Lou, Tausk was seduced by her in no time at all. Whatever her motives, it was a clever move on her part, which for a while at least made her indispensable both to Tausk and to Freud. More interestingly from our point of view, she provides an illuminating – and notably level-headed – account, not only of the relationship between the two men, but of the source of many of Freud's difficulties with his colleagues and of the manner of their progression.

When she returned to Göttingen she began to treat her own analytic patients, despite the fact that, unlike the vast majority of Freud's colleagues, she had never been analysed – had never, as far as we know, even thought of it. It wasn't long before she'd become one of the *grandes dames* of psychoanalysis – a figure to be reckoned with. Although 'die Lou', as Alix Strachey called her, didn't agree with Freud in every respect – she was a nineteenth-century optimist where he was a twentieth-century pessimist – her journal enables us, maybe uniquely, to see how his ideas were received and accommodated by a member of the contemporary intelligentsia. It isn't always easy to read – the mistiness of its prose, too, is very much of its time – but the effort is well repaid: there aren't many other informal accounts of the emotional strains and intellectual pleasures involved in being a part of Freud's circle. The journal wasn't published in her lifetime – she died in 1937 – but it's unlikely, given the obsessive loyalty of her executors, that she didn't intend it at some point to see the light of day. She had no doubt that her own ideas, however modest in relation to Freud's, deserved to be known and taken seriously.

Mary-Kay Wilmers

TRANSLATOR'S INTRODUCTION

Lou Andreas-Salomé will probably always be remembered best for her friendships, notably for those with Nietzsche, Rilke, and Freud. The sheer weight of the names ensures her vicarious immortality; who else could have been even slightly acquainted with all three? The apposition of the philosopher, the poet, and the psychoanalyst in the life and memories of one woman suggests her uniqueness of character. Hers was no borrowed luster. There existed such interaction between the woman and each of the three men that her spirit may be found to have insinuated itself into the writings of all of them. Hence we turn with interest to the first of her journals to be published and look in it for the fresh record of great meetings.

Even the most intimate of private journals seems to presuppose the eventual attention of a second reader. This one has about it the note of address to an audience which implies that it was designed for publication, at least in part, and we must assume that the author's critical eye attended it. It was kept in a little red loose-leaf notebook which escaped the Nazis, who after her death in 1937 presumed to purge her library. For the most part it is a record of her studies with Freud and his pupils, but the remarkable fact of the record is that the student approached her teacher as a respectful equal, never doubting that the experiences of her own life could serve as criteria for the validity of the findings of the great discoverer.

The same judicious independence of thought is in the journal
when it turns from the circle of doctors around Freud—and
from the rival circle newly started around Alfred Adler—to her
other friends. She was enough at ease in philosophy to look
shrewdly at Max Scheler, and she felt confident enough of her
insights in psychoanalysis to investigate the dreams of Rilke, narrated to her as they walked together in the mountains. She pro-
pounded theories of the function of the cinema in modern life, of
the heroic ballad in the primitive Slavonic world, of the baroque
in art. If we are not always convinced, we are nonetheless impressed by the seriousness and boldness of the mental enterprise
and the imaginativeness which shakes off the bonds of preconcep-
tion.

In this journal, as might be expected from its focus on the
work and person of Sigmund Freud, the psychoanalytic atmosphere is everywhere. To the psychoanalyst the writings of Lou
Andreas-Salomé are a strange world, where familiar words appear
in the most unexpected connections and where familiar concepts
have undergone a transformation that is often delightful, often
perplexing, and always surprising. In this rare instance, the clinical
observer and theorist was also a poet and novelist, who alter-
nated between poetic ambiguity and psychological preciseness
and sometimes mixed the two. Reading her for the first time, as
in this journal, we are frequently struck by how her psychoanalytic thinking differs in this respect from that of others among
Freud's early followers. Not that the poetic vision is rare among
them. Perhaps it is only by a slight developmental turn that an
individual becomes a psychoanalyst and not a writer, and, in their
best writing, analysts often turn to living images to represent
their thoughts. But the clinical scientist speedily regains the upper hand, and the image is domesticated to the rigorous demands
of logic. In the long run it is the business of psychoanalysis to
interpret the dreams we are made of and not, like poetry, to interpret life in the language of the dream.

Lou Andreas-Salomé was fifty years old when she came into first-hand contact with psychoanalysis, although she had known Freud's writings earlier. She brought with her, first to the Weimar Congress in 1911 and then to Vienna the following year, all she had thought and dreamed until then; for her the discovery of psychoanalysis was a discovery of what she had always known. It was Freud's "Christmas present" to her, as he remarked, according to her account here. The gift must have been a semantic bridge between the unconscious life of the emotions about which she had been writing all her life and the philosophical synthesis toward which she had aspired.

She wrote of the meeting with Freud and his colleagues as the "turning point" of her life, and it had been a life of dramatic crises and dénouements. Objectively this was the turning point in that she spent her remaining twenty-five years as a psychoanalyst, treating patients at her home, "Loufried," in Göttingen, and writing a small number of papers about psychoanalysis. More important perhaps for her own life was the conviction she had gained that she now understood many things which had hitherto only aroused her sympathetic wonder, such as the extraordinary mind of Rainer Maria Rilke, so intimately a part of her own personal experience, yet so incomprehensible in its heights and its lapses. The psychology of religion also—the subject of her first psychoanalytic essay,[1] but of many earlier writings as well—seemed to yield its secret to analysis; her own mysticism, divested of traditional religious faith when she was a girl, now had a firm intellectual basis in the theory of the unconscious. And not least was her earning through psychoanalysis (although she was apparently never analyzed herself) a higher degree of emotional integration, an approach to the unity and serenity which Freud considered to be hers.

She was born in St. Petersburg in 1861 and named Louise Salomé. She was the sixth child and only daughter of a former general in the Imperial Russian Army. Both her parents were the descendants of German Protestants long established in the Baltic provinces and northern Germany. The family name was French, deriving, it was said, from French Huguenot *émigrés* to Germany. She was the darling of her elderly father, himself an impressive figure around whom her early religiosity centered.

While still a girl she began keeping notebooks, which have not been published. Like other future writers she wrote down the thoughts of her youth, and these notebooks were the source of many of the ideas which she developed in her later writings. The present volume is a continuation of the girlhood journals, and like them it contains in preliminary form many of the ideas—in this case psychoanalytic ideas—which she later wrote about more extensively. Again as with many writers, there was a spontaneous self-therapeutic purpose in the keeping of her journals. The written word gives substance to the evanescent stuff of fantasy, and at the same time is a link to the world of other persons; nothing has ever been written that did not presuppose the existence of a reader, for whom a real language needed to be chosen. For all her privileged position in the household and in society she was also—as she has described in her memoirs and her stories—an isolated, lonely child, much given to daydreaming and not always able to discriminate her fantasies from her external life. She told about this part of her childhood in her autobiography,[2] written in old age, and some of her stories too were drawn from memories of it. The primitive sense of relatedness to objects, live or inanimate, certainly universal in childhood, had an exceptional dominance in her case—so much so that, for example, the melting of a pair of snow images,[3] endowed by her with living personalities, induced in her a feeling of "God's departure" which shook the foundations of her psychic life. Even if we are correct in recognizing a screen memory in this recollection, a summary in distorted form of repressed memories and ideas, it points to the origins of a life in which fantasy was ever nearby and familiar.

The possessor of an intensely vivid inner world of fantasy—or the one "possessed" by such a world, it might be more accurate to say—has reason to require of life that it conform to the demands of this very special, very private existence. Lou Andreas-Salomé, many years later, told the young Anna Freud[4] that the only "sin" was to be untrue to one's own nature. To live it was for her to fulfill her unique destiny and hence to represent truly that aspect of the universe of nature which had its being in her. The ideal of self-realization can of course be a philosophical mask for undisclosed conflicts like any other ideal. It is certainly true that the course of Lou Salomé's life was one of ceaseless determination to be true to her image of herself and to reject all influences that might have limited her. Her departure from Russia as a girl of nineteen came as a consequence of this determination or of the unconscious ideas that lay within it.

A few years before she had turned for guidance, intellectual as well as spiritual, to a Dutch Reformed pastor in St. Petersburg—Hendrik Gillot. This man—more than twice her age, married, and the father of a family—took charge of her education from that time, with the somewhat reluctant consent of her mother. Gillot had a considerable knowledge of literature and philosophy as well as of theology, and he directed Lou Salomé's reading at a level well beyond her years. The atmosphere of mutual devotion to learning inevitably had erotic overtones, and it is a little hard to believe that Gillot's proposal of marriage came as the complete surprise she alleged it to be. Yet it might have been so, since it is likely that many years passed before she accepted herself as a sexual being. At any rate, she refused Gillot, and soon afterward, in poor health, she went with her mother to Zürich and from there to Rome.

She was twenty-one when she reached Rome, still not quite well, and when Paul Rée, a young philosopher, introduced her to Friedrich Nietzsche. This meeting, carefully prepared by Rée, took place in St. Peter's Cathedral. It was to have been the beginning of a partnership of three, including a plan to live the student life together. Nietzsche was much older than Lou Salomé, thirty-eight, but he had heard of the brilliant Russian and imagined her a kindred spirit, one whom he hoped to bring up as his disciple. His initial greeting in the cathedral set the tone: "From what stars have we fallen to meet here?" The details of this idyll have been preserved in Lou Salomé's own version in her autobiography and with some modifications in Peters' biography of her. It has about it the tragic and ironic element that colored Nietzsche's life and doctrine, and yet it cannot but strike the modern reader as a little comic, too, in its vociferous romanticism. For more than a year such a succession of passionate invocations and operatic posturings went on that it is easy to forget its significance for all the tormented participants.

For Lou Salomé it offered an unforgettable insight into the mind of the great philosopher, who poured out his ideas along with his love. For him, it was a longed-for, nearly despaired-of break in his loneliness. He hoped to find with Lou Salomé a new and happy beginning. She "was prepared like none other for that part of my philosophy that has hardly yet been uttered." [5] But not only did the disciple remain elusive; Nietzsche's mother and his madly jealous sister violently opposed his relationship with her and said she had openly mocked him and his declarations of love, even talking about them with his one-time friend Richard Wagner. Nietzsche hoped for a reconciliation with Lou Salomé, even after her refusal was final and after his subsequent depression. As late as 1884, he said of her: "I have never known a more gifted or more understanding creature." He attributed to her influence the immense enhancement of his productive powers in the year he was associated with her. When her novel *In Kampf um Gott* appeared in 1885 he wrote of its brilliance. But his loss of her proved to him that he was to find no woman to rescue him from his loneliness.

Nothing is more characteristic of the complexity of Lou Salomé's personality than the circumstances of her marriage to Friedrich Carl Andreas in 1887. Although she had long since left Nietzsche, she had remained close to his friend and hers, Paul Rée, and Rée was surprised and deeply injured at the marriage. Andreas, already a distinguished student of Near Eastern languages and many years older than Lou Salomé, induced her to marry him by attempting suicide. She wrote at length, and at her most oblique—for she could be misleadingly allusive—of Andreas and the marriage, in her autobiography. It was not a sexual union, and Andreas must have been another in the series of men, like Gillot, whom she admired and respected as fathers rather than as lovers.

It is unnecessary here to recount in detail the names of the many men whom Lou Andreas-Salomé knew as fathers, lovers, and friends. Her autobiography is in its way a model of discretion, but its hints are in places unmistakable and provocative. As for her journals and letters, which have provided much more information than her published writings, we know that they were bequeathed to the friend of her old age, Ernst Pfeiffer and that their publication was authorized. From what we know of her it is not difficult to suspect that she would have accepted with good grace the prospect of the ultimate publication of the history of her loves. It is only one of the fascinating complexities of her personality that she was discreet in her conversation—and only slightly less so in some of her writings—and yet, no doubt, would have accepted the modern convention that the sexual history of noted individuals is in the public domain.

Not only the famous names that we encounter arouse our interest, but their significance in the life of one whose views on love and marriage, on the relations of the sexes in general, have been so fully stated. The names are impressive enough, the list reading like a résumé of the continental literary life circa 1900. Nietzsche's judgment as to her extraordinary capacities for understanding seems to have been shared by dozens of men and women for whom the intellect, the word, have importance. Gerhart Hauptmann, Jakob Wassermann, Martin Buber, Richard Beer-Hofmann, Frank Wedekind, Arthur Schnitzler, Marie von Ebner-Eschenbach were only a few of them. Of most significance to her was Rainer Maria Rilke, to whose life and destiny this journal often refers.

To follow Lou Andreas-Salomé's ideas about love, marriage, and fidelity, it is necessary to know that all her life she resisted the position of domesticity and motherhood which accompanies monogamous existence, which indeed for most women makes monogamy not only endurable but highly desirable. Her accounting for her behavior, usually put in general rather than specific terms, is also so involved and apparently rationalized that it is not only the psychoanalyst who reads it with skepticism. We can accept as sincere her determination to be true to herself and her conviction that an unqualified devotion to one man was physically repugnant, a spiritual slavery. What arouses our skepticism is her attempt in some places to make a kind of ethical norm out of her own life of serial polyandry, which must strike us as a compulsive life and anything but a general human possibility. It was as if the continued presence of a lover were bound eventually to bore her with that ennui that is always based on anxiety. Nor need this speculation be considered very farfetched: in her "Thoughts on the Problem of Love" [6] she attributes the power of love to the strangeness, the novelty of the lovers to each other, and she precedes this with some remarks on the universality of the incest taboo. A profound insight for 1900, when this paper was published, but, insofar as it reveals anything about the writer, the association is diagnostic of neurotic sexuality. She required the repeated reassurance which only a new lover could give her. Worldly recognition for her talents as a writer—and she became well known as novelist and essayist—did not fulfill her need for the devotion of an unlimited number of men. And she obtained it; men sought and found her love well into the sixth decade of her life.

She was a *femme fatale*. Men longed for her, suffered for her, and it is possible that one or two even died for her. She herself looked on Paul Rée's death in a mountaineering accident as linked with his loss of her, although it occurred many years after her marriage with Andreas. About Victor Tausk's suicide in 1919 she wrote[7] to Freud in a dispassionate, almost clinical, tone, which demands comparison with her comments about him in this journal. She was possibly also one of those women whom Freud had in mind when he wrote that their characters were indelibly marked by the men who had been their lovers. What is more pertinent is that her lovers (and her friends, such as Freud) were influenced by her, their lives and ideas bearing the stamp of her presence. In some instances she gave ideas to them; in others it must have been more her sympathetic listening and her extraordinary power of penetrating to meanings of which they were themselves unaware; and in still others, such as Rilke's life, it was her existence as an unshakable personality which could lend of its substance to encourage, support, direct.

Although Nietzsche's philosophy and character most influenced her still-formative years, and it was Freud who determined the final course of her life, Rainer Maria Rilke was the genius who seems to have been never far from her thoughts. She was thirty-six, he twenty-one, when they met in Munich—a reversal of the disparity in age so evident before. Rilke had already a literary reputation, although his great work lay in the future. His attention had been called to her by her essay "Jesus the Jew," [8] in which he recognized a spirit akin to that of his own "Christus-Visionen." He courted her with letters and poems after their meeting, and he won her love. The passionate affair which followed lasted several years, including two journeys together to Russia, on one of which they were accompanied by Andreas, and the affair was followed by a friendship that lasted until Rilke's death. A large volume of their correspondence has been published[9]—to be sure a rather one-sided correspondence with much more of Rilke than of Lou in it—and she also wrote an

appreciative memoir of Rilke after his death. In the present journal we see the friendship of sixteen years or so subjected to a
new scrutiny, that of psychoanalysis. Lou Andreas-Salomé was
by this time—as the journal makes plain—a thoroughgoing disciple of Freud, and like his other pupils she saw the world with
new eyes made sensitive to unconscious and symbolic meanings.
Whether psychoanalytic interpretation of this kind could really
penetrate the mystery of the poet's soul is another matter. In a
way we learn most about the nature of the creative process in
Rilke's experience from the schematic annotations which she
wrote down after his visit to her in Göttingen in July 1913, his
recollections of his travels, which later found their way into his
Duino Elegies and the *Sonnets to Orpheus*. The recounting of
these incidents to Lou may have equipped the poet with a firmer
basis for their elaboration into poetry. From his dreams and fantasies and her interpretations of them, we learn more about the
neurotic than the creative process—more, that is, about what is
common to all men than what is peculiar to genius. And in a significant detail the analyst herself expressed her doubts about further analyzing this delicately integrated poet. Yet from Rilke's own
letters and poems we can be certain that he found both inspiration and nurture in this great listener.

There is enough about Rilke in the journal to throw light on
the nature of the relationship between him and Lou. She was
here as always in her self-disclosures in the dominant position,
and there is only a faint trace of any erotic longing, as when she
contemplated the sandals he had left behind. For the most part
she was engaged in fostering the sick soul she saw in him, to
rescue him from the neuroticism which she thought always endangered his creativity. She was a mother in her concern for him
and also a therapist—hardly a desirable combination of roles
and perhaps especially so here where neither was free of con-
descension. Yet the deeper layer of the text betrays her wonder
at the unaccountable poetic power of the man, which had pro-

gressed so far from his early days to the present, from the relatively simple lyrical outbursts of the past, which included a little volume celebrating their love, to his newest work, in which intensely experienced details were complexly woven into new universes of allusion.

A great listener she was—and this, too, may have had its dark side. In the company of one or two she could speak with vigor and clarity, but she was oppressed in some way by larger groups. She tells us in the journal what she might have said in Freud's circle, but her silence was bred not solely of respect for the talents of the men in the room; she was far more talented than many of them. It was anxiety that silenced her, but so complex a person was she that there must have been no outward manifestation of her anxiety; instead she showed the welcoming, receptive, eager comprehension which was more seductive than any words, or so we are permitted to infer from the outcome. Victor Tausk loved her, and Freud was "spellbound" by her empty chair when she was absent one day from his course, having become habituated to address his remarks to her. Yet it is to lose sight of the essential thing to emphasize too much the seductive side of her personality. She had other qualities to justify her admission to this select group.

Her writings were then well known to readers of contemporary German literature. In addition to her novels, her books on Nietzsche and Ibsen, and her short stories, she had published many articles and reviews, especially on religion, drama, sexuality, the psychology of women—all topics that come up in this journal for reconsideration in the light of psychoanalysis. Her writings were intensely personal, and this was to be true also of the psychoanalytic papers of her later life. Her own memories, fantasies, and emotions were either transformed into the artistic form of fiction or directed her attention to philosophic and aesthetic ideas which she brought to life with them. Her writing drew on her own experience in an immediate way. If she lacked objectivity, she was also incapable of the cliché, and having grasped the essence of philosophic speculations or scientific observations, she presented them in her own manner.

At times a price has to be paid for this by the reader. Her encompassing interest, plus a drive to express all the elaborate complexity of her own response to whatever she learned, often resulted in labored and turgid prose. The German language is dangerously susceptible to abuse of this kind; the cumulative, overupholstered sentences, with dependent clauses hanging by their teeth through the subtleties of inflected relative pronouns, can lead in the end to less rather than more clarity. The poetical idea is sometimes dimmed in a forest of abstract associations or attenuated in a solution of allusions. While in her stories and her essays on religion and love, for example, Lou Andreas-Salomé could express her original thoughts with relative simplicity, theoretical ideas derived from psychoanalysis were often convoluted and redundant. One thing she did not learn from Freud was the mastery of unequivocal utterance.

Lou Andreas-Salomé came to Vienna to devote herself to "all phases" of psychoanalysis at a particularly dramatic time in the life of this movement. The *Minutes of the Vienna Psychoanalytic Society* for the years 1906 to 1908[10] (the only volume published so far) reveal plain signs of the open dissension that was to follow. Personal antagonisms played a large part in these dissensions. Psychoanalysis attracted, among others, neurotic men who had the courage to recognize their abnormality, but not necessarily the wisdom to see its consequences in their human relations. They could not see that some of their theoretical differences acquired exaggerated significance because of their own egoism, or, as Freud was convinced, their resistance to insight. The *Minutes* also point to the startling crudity of arguments *ad hominem* that were often used by the protagonists in debate. Nothing is very new about this in arguments, including those that scientists engage in, and it is naïve, if understandable, to expect that all those engaged in the psychological treatment of their fellow-humans will pursue a uniformly high-minded course.

When the dissensions came to be revolutions, another cause than personal differences needs to be admitted. Freud had opened the way into a new realm of thought: no references to "the unconscious before Freud," to all the brilliant insights by his predecessors, or to the innumerable glimpses into the unconscious life which constitute so much of the poetic, artistic, and religious vision, in any way dispute Freud's priority. The realm turns out to be infinitely various, however, as the world of nature always does. The concepts by which it was initially grasped were not wrong, but they were insufficient. Freud spent his life in constant elaborations and refinements of his concepts, but it was to be expected that even in his lifetime radical oppositions of emphasis would occur.

We can dismiss Stekel's break with Freud easily; witness Freud's words in a letter to Ludwig Binswanger: "His jealousy has become limitless, and his self-esteem exaggerated to the point of being grotesque." [11] In the cases of Adler and Jung it is not so easy. In a way, Jung's position toward psychoanalysis around 1912 is analogous to the position of vitalism in biology. It was a move from one set of explanatory concepts to another, which effectively undermined the first. It was not an addition to or an extension of Freud's theories, but one which made them unnecessary. If, with our analogy, we look on biological science as derived from the physicochemical explanation of living processes, we will not expect much help from a vitalistic system which requires an unanalyzable "entelechy." So Jung did not simply claim that Freud's explanatory concept of sexuality for example was inadequate—as indeed it proved to be—he introduced a "libido" which was inherently transcendent and inexplicable. As Lou Andreas-Salomé asserts, a premature philosophical synthesis was thus attained, a monistic synthesis which does not explain but eliminates psychic conflict.

Adler also succeeded in disposing to his own satisfaction of the

fundamental emphasis placed by Freud on sexuality. His theory
of fictions appealed to her, but she saw, as the journal shows, the
absurdities to which the theory led in Adler's hands. Other aspects
of Adler's ideas, understood in retrospect, might have offered necessary corrections and amplifications to psychoanalytic theory—
his recognition of the aggressive drive, for example, and his grasp
of social experience as a source of the subterfuges of the ego. The
dissensions were not only questions of personality and philosophy,
but also of timing.

They were important in themselves, but they were also the beginnings of the "schools of psychoanalysis" which have developed alongside Freud's teachings, with the latter acquiring the
ambiguous merit of "orthodoxy." Lou Andreas-Salomé's observations of Freud in action will help the reader decide for himself to
what extent the discoverer was intolerant of new ideas from his
followers. They gave him trouble; of that there is no doubt.
They could falsify the theories, they could press them beyond
the capacity of their observations to bear them, or they could
tread so closely on Freud's heels that he was forced to premature statements. Often he wished he were alone; yet his ability to
react affirmatively to their stimulations is also evident. Their
gifts were various—Rank, Ferenczi, and Tausk being most prominent among them—and none of them were blind followers. Karl
Abraham, working in Berlin, is barely mentioned in the journal,
but he contributed as much as anyone to the progress of the
work. It is worthwhile to consider how much his colleagues
brought to Freud's attention that he might otherwise have
missed. He always acknowledged his debts—including a major
debt to Lou Andreas-Salomé herself—but one never gets the impression that in Vienna or elsewhere major scientific advances
were made by groups or committees.

Meanwhile, in the background as far as the journal is concerned, the year 1912-1913 had independent significance in the
history of Freud's ideas, independent that is of the secessions.

His major works, the two pioneering volumes which had established the foundations of the science were well behind him—namely the *Interpretation of Dreams* (1900) and the *Three Essays on the Theory of Sexuality* (1905). The former volume is the great demonstration of the empirical data on which Freud's theories were based, and in its seventh chapter the outline of the theoretical system is drawn. The *Three Essays* gave to the concept of sexuality its elaboration to include a wide variety of seemingly unrelated psychic functions. The two books had an encyclopedic scope, but the scientific hypotheses in them could only give rise to innumerable new questions. Some of these led to the schools, but others, or even the same ones at times, led to new investigations.

A recent study of Freud's had been his work on the memoirs of the psychotic jurist Daniel Paul Schreber. In addition, he was publishing the separate chapters of his major excursion into anthropology, *Totem and Taboo*. These were studies of books, not patients; the first was the analysis of a schizophrenic on the basis of the patient's own writings, the second a psychoanalytic interpretation of the mental life of primitive peoples as recorded in anthropological works of the time, and then compared by Freud with the mental life of children and neurotics. From these two aspects and with another more directly clinical consideration also in mind—the psychoanalysis of homosexuality—a fundamental innovation was in sight which was to be the subject of much more detailed comment in a paper still in process of being formulated—the problem of narcissism.

Without the specific designation, the problem of narcissism was an old one for Lou Andreas-Salomé. The psychology of love must include the psychology of self-love, and the rivalry between love and self-love is an implicit problem of life even when unrecognized. Between the person and the object of his love the self intervenes in many disguises. In women especially, she thought, the aim of love is to expand the self, not to strive for a distant goal, as the romantic man does in his pursuit of the ever-desirable, because unattainable, woman. The love of God is the complete self-love by this view, since we create out of ourselves a perfected image which we adore and to which we submit. But she was also concerned about a deeper kind of self-love, and this concern originated in her own personal mysticism of union. If the self and the other person, or the self and the whole of nature somehow exist in a primal union, then separation into full individuality has never occurred, and love is in effect, as in the old Platonic myth, the rediscovery of a lost part of the self.

While Lou Andreas-Salomé came to the study of narcissism from her thoughts about woman, love, and God, Freud had other problems in mind. He had found out early in his career as an analyst that a difference between neurotic and psychotic patients lay in the fact that the latter did not have the same capacity as the former to turn their emotional interest, and in a significant degree their love, to the analyst. Instead it appeared that the psychotics held on to their love and took themselves as its object. Their own thoughts, words, and feelings totally engaged their attention; unlike neurotics they had abandoned even fantasies of other persons than themselves. In the psychotic state of megalomania, they endowed themselves with exalted qualities and virtues. But there is a megalomania of another sort, not limited to psychotics. Primitive people, untutored in the sophistications of logic, are struck by the apparent efficacy of their own words, their charms, their magic of all kinds to bring about desired or undesired ends. The mind's ability to create worlds out of fantasy is a wonder that ever attracts us to turn back on ourselves, especially when the world of external persons and other objects fails to satisfy. So, too, children have side by side with their helplessness the illusory conviction of their ability to control their parents and the whole of the external world through the mere wishing and the mere command.

Freud's concept of narcissism, as he published it in his 1914 essay, provided Lou Salomé with a theoretical explanation of the vicissitudes of self-love, but it is noteworthy that this is one of several topics on which her agreement with Freud was always a good deal less than complete. Her writings about narcissism emphasize the side of it that interested her most—the primary state of the as yet undifferentiated self—and she came back often in her later work to the image of the mother and child, the unborn or newly born child. Freud and his followers have attributed great importance to the very early period of postnatal life, but on account of the scarcity of verifiable data have avoided interpretations based on it. If, however, the experiences of certain withdrawn, regressed psychotics and of some of the mystics and poets that especially concerned Lou Salomé are relevant to early infantile narcissism, then consideration of it is demanded.

The journal foreshadows other subsequent psychoanalytic writings. As always, these were based on interests which she had had long before she came to know about psychoanalysis, in fact in some cases before it existed. The psychology of the poet Rilke is one of the topics of her later work *Mein Dank an Freud*.[12] Also the journal anticipates, in one passage in particular, her study of the ideas "anal" and "sexual," a study which Freud looked on as a major contribution to analytic theory. In addition to its analysis of the stage of development accompanying the period of toilet training, it touches on the specific psychology of woman, a subject to which she also devoted a psychoanalytic paper. Yet all of these sound one way or another the recurrent note of that primary, undisturbed, peaceful union which she attributed to early infancy, when the struggle between the instincts and the ego had not yet begun.

She was such an apt student that her teachers appear to have grown wiser in her presence, but she gave no one unqualified agreement. The journal records many instances of the difficulties she saw in psychoanalysis. Some of these were inherent in the psychoanalytic process, but they revealed major philosophical issues. Turning directly to Nietzsche, the great existentialist, she foresaw a problem which has been voiced in the existentialist criticism of our day: the "unalterable contradiction in the application of a method derived from science—the logical analysis by which we gain control of the outer world—to the immediate data of our inmost experiences." Wisely she saw this difficulty not as an obstacle to psychoanalytic theory, as do the later existentialists, but as the source of resistance in all patients, who inevitably project on psychoanalysis as such that fragmentation of their psychic unity which actually constitutes their illness. She doubtless lived long enough to know the contrary problem of psychoanalysis, the all-too-eager intellectualistic defense, whereby theory, usually in a degraded or popularized form, is used by patients as a resistance against exposure to the "immediate data" of experience, which are all the analyst wants to hear.

The language of psychoanalysis had its difficulties too, she thought. It was too stark, too coarse, not in the sense that it was shocking, but in its omission of the finer gradations of feeling-tones. Here it is the poet-novelist who is speaking against the reductive tendency, the one-sidedness which ignores the ego's elaborations of primitive inclinations. She also protested against the instinct theory itself insofar as it seemed to beg the question by reference to an organic substrate—for just what do we say about the instincts when we claim for them a physical matrix which stands in a causal relation to them? The age-old philosophical problem of how the material, quantifiable objective structure of physical reality becomes mental is unanswered by Freud too. Not that she could propose a solution. Instead, by way of Spinoza she attacks the question itself, which presumes that there actually *is* a series of which one member is body and another is mind. Her critique of Adler's theory of organ inferiority has a similar philosophical basis: the psychological realm has its own organization and its own laws. Some of her warnings have a startling pertinence to present issues in psychoanalysis. The desire to close the gap that presumably exists between mental and physical processes turns ever again to premature or irrelevant bridges. Cerebral localization is far advanced today beyond its state fifty years ago, but its usefulness as a support for psychoanalytic theory may still be a wish-fulfillment, now as then proceeding from our anxiety over the reality of mind.

Her stay in Vienna naturally had its personal side. She learned by telegram of the death of her mother in Russia. She called on old friends like Richard Beer-Hofmann and Marie von Ebner-Eschenbach. She went to the movies and reflected on their aesthetic and social meaning, and she found a new lover in Victor Tausk. Tausk, next to Freud and the author herself, appears in the journal as the most lively figure. The "beast-of-prey," as Freud called him, was presenting a course of his own on psychoanalysis which Lou attended. His unhappy marriage had recently dissolved, and he welcomed her attachment to him and his little boys. Once again the outcome was foreseeable. Tausk had "fantasies" of a permanent love, and with her strange independence and hardness, she separated from him.

Our picture of Freud is not likely to be substantially altered by the account of him in the journal. His confidence and his humor are familiar to us, as is the pessimistic turn of mind that contrasted with Lou Andreas-Salomé's optimism, her "intoxication with life—a little of which beneficially circulates in the blood and brain of healthy men," as she wrote in a later paper. In her autobiography she recalled Freud's wry reply to her early poem "Hymn to Life," mistakenly attributed by him to Nietzsche, who had composed a musical setting for it. When she expressed in it her wish to live forever, enduring whatever pain life might bring, Freud answered that a bad cold would cure him of such a desire. She takes us a step into Freud's inner world also in her observations on his position toward his colleagues. He was grateful indeed for their loyalty and their inspiration, but their ill-advised advances on his work could harass him as much as their quarrels.

The sympathetic little details Lou Salomé noted do bring Freud closer to our understanding—his escorting her home, his keen comment on the devoted Otto Rank, the story of the "narcissistic cat."

Much later, in a letter dated May 1931,[13] Freud wrote to Lou Andreas-Salomé of "your superiority over all of us—in accord with the heights from which you descended to us." It is only one of his tributes to her and was specifically related there to her ability to synthesize analytic data "back again into a living organism." In a way such a tribute to a friend was not unusual for Freud. One of the sides of his personality was the capacity for boundless respect for those who could accept his discoveries and make them into something of their own. This stands out in his relations with those of his followers who held to philosophic positions quite contrary to his own. Lou was one of these, Binswanger and Pfister were others, as his letters to them plainly reveal.[14,15] It is interesting that he wrote to Binswanger, also at a much later time,[16] that he himself had "always dwelt only in the ground floor and basement of the buildings," that he did not live in the "upper stories in which such distinguished guests as religion, art, etc., reside." Here the conscious ambivalence of his attitude is clearer. Freud was at once aware of an orientation toward life that was not his own, the lack of which might be a deficiency of his, while mistrustful of those "heights" as regions perilously close to the realm of illusion. Just as he was always concerned with religion and art and often wrote about them, so also in his positivistic evaluation of them they did not have the merit of science. Lou Salomé had the peculiar power to reflect the aura of her "superiority" without disparaging the "basement" world of the instincts. And of course hers was not simply a philosophical attitude; the association of spirituality and eroticism was integral and all-pervasive in her.

After Vienna and her stay in Budapest to work with Ferenczi, her visit from Rilke at Göttingen and their later tour of the Riesengebirge in Silesia, the Munich Congress in 1913 when the Swiss analysts, led by Jung made their graceless departure, and after a number of jottings on other illustrious figures, the journal ends fittingly on a religious note, returning to one of her oldest concerns, "God the Father." Fittingly for our time, the great figures of Abu Simbel dominating the landscape are the last to be seen.

Lou Andreas-Salomé lived until 1937. The last third of her life, the psychoanalytic third, was outwardly much less eventful than the first part. One wonders whether psychoanalysis was itself responsible for the change or only the growing conservatism of age. A friend asked her during this epoch whether she regretted not having known about analysis in her youth, had it existed then. She smiled and said that she would not like to have missed all the follies she had committed when she was young. Somehow her reply fits with the comment we find in the journal that she had not come to analysis because of any conflict "between the surface and the depths." It is hard to believe, but it appears that she believed it.

In the long period in Göttingen, she practiced psychoanalysis and wrote many papers and books. Her house, situated on a high hill outside the town, was a substantial one with a large garden of flowers, fruits, and vegetables, and she assisted in caring for them. The house and garden provided both shelter and isolation for the oddly mated couple who lived there. Andreas continued, until his death in 1930, in his professorship at the university, but neither he nor she participated in the social life of the town and the faculty. Its bourgeois stuffiness and class-consciousness were quite foreign to their nature. When World War I came, the income from the Russian family ceased, and in the hardest time, when fuel was too costly for work in the evenings, Freud saw to it that funds were made available to his old friend.[17]

The correspondence of Freud and Lou Andreas-Salomé has

been preserved.[18] Her early efforts at analyzing patients—including some by mail—were encouraged by Freud. Her extensive and sometimes elaborate theorizings were rather less welcome, and his replies likely to be brief. He deplored her need to bring about a philosophic synthesis based on analysis. But he also shared many of his problems and worries with her. In one amusing exchange, he puzzled about her addressing an envelope to him in which her husband's initials were substituted for his; her reply was not a revealing one.

The analytic studies written during this time are quickly enumerated, but less easily summarized. She began with a little paper on a childhood religious experience.[19] Here she turned to her own recollections—which may have been fantasies too—of incidents connected with her father and seemingly representing the unity of omnipotence and love. She derived from them and their infantile meaning assurance of a kind of deified grandfather readily identified with the Christian God of her upbringing, but in a very special private relationship to her as the objective guarantor of the reality of her own fantasies and of her own rectitude. For it was a secret alliance of the child and God against the injustices of the adult world.

In the second paper, one on femininity,[20] she rested her ideas—as always—on personal experience, and she did not leave far behind her earlier, pre-Freudian studies in sexuality. She simply reviewed these studies in the light of psychoanalytic knowledge, amplified and modified them somewhat, but once again made it plain that analysis confirmed and clarified what she had intuitively always known. In fact, her thesis and her method are interrelated: in a woman's life reality is recognized as something received, or even conceived, within herself, not something which she seeks. She is open to new experience, but it is revelatory of what already exists. Feminine sexuality is always closer to the original union, less given to aggressive drives, and less isolated from its sublimatory expressions than male sexuality. In her conception of the child, in childbearing and childrearing the woman produces the replica of herself, as the creative artist does with his work. All this she had stated without reference to psychoanalysis in her paper called—untranslatably—"Der Mensch als Weib" [21] fifteen years before. Woman is thus, in her view, the antithesis of Faustian man; she does not pursue the unattainable, the infinite. Why should she, being herself the goal, *das Ewig-Weibliche*?

In her work on "Anality and Sexuality," [22] published in 1916, she came closest to writing like other psychoanalysts, and it is this study which Freud summarized in a later edition of his *Three Essays on Sexuality*,[23] where he referred to it as "a paper which has given us a very much deeper understanding of the significance of anal erotism." She showed there how the first prohibition the child must encounter—the prohibition of pleasure in anal activity—confronts him with an external world hitherto hardly defined as such and now revealed as hostile to his impulses. At the same time that he must separate himself from the environment, he must also repress a valuable part of himself. It is repudiation, first from without and then from within, that differentiates the ego from the drives. Whatever is anal symbolizes from then on that which must be excluded. The proximity of the anal zone to the genital, which in the woman "is only leased" from it, endows the latter apparatus with permanent anal meanings. It is the approving judgment of the sexual partner which alone can liberate sex from shame and guilt.

I have already remarked on her paper "The Dual Orientation of Narcissism" [24] in which she at length discussed how she found in Freud's hypotheses confirmation of her own, already articulated in a different language. It was not, however, in the easy way that speculative thinkers often gain a spurious merit by claiming for their own ideas the validity which scientists have achieved by hard work. The singular, sometimes monotonous, unity of her thoughts on narcissism had both experiential and philosophic roots. In a late work, the little book published on the occasion of Freud's seventy-fifth birthday,[25] she recalled an episode from Rilke's Duino period in which the poet tried to put into prose words his feelings of at-oneness with the tree which confronted him and the gradual emergence of the experience into poetic form. The poet, the artist, is no illusionist, she wrote, but rather "he lays hold of his sense experience out of primitive impressions in which world and man are for him undifferentiated reality and it is this which he *realizes* in his work."

The problem of narcissism was thus for her the problem of creativity—and creativity was never very distant in her mind from femininity. The lover of many men had at times an oddly condescending attitude toward maleness. The masculine principle, even as God, was for her woman's own creation—or the artist's, which psychologically came to the same thing. That the magnificence of this creation must have derived from the little girl's contemplation of her splendid father of long ago only points to the source of her profound ambivalence, which in turn has something to do with the complicatedness of her ideas.

Creativity too has a resemblance to the pathological, since both come from the nonrational levels. The ego must relax its hold for either to come into being—art or disease. The pathological is a lapse, a passive submission to unconscious forces, so that Rilke, for example, could come to believe in the existence beyond himself of the "angels" he had himself created. This is the opposite tendency from the creative effort of the poet. In the latter case he is not at the mercy of his fantasies, because they are not erotized for him. They retain their original foothold in the most primitive phases, in which subject and object are barely discriminated; and yet they pursue pathways away from mere discharge as sexual wish-fulfillments.

In her last decade, she wrote little directly connected with psychoanalysis, although it was her constant occupation. In her autobiography, which was published posthumously, she returned to her friendship with Freud and movingly recounted their last meeting. The final years of her life were spent in great loneliness, for the German people had become infected with the delusions of their psychotic master, and Freud's former pupil was open to suspicion. The great hoard of letters, books, and journals was guarded by her and entrusted at her death to Ernst Pfeiffer, one of the few companions of her old age; the original publication of this journal is a fruit of that friendship.

In the obituary note that Freud wrote on her death,[26] he described Lou Andreas-Salomé as one beyond human frailty. It is impossible to know whether he was ever exposed to the bewildering manifoldness of her character, ranging behind the manifest wholeness. In the quarter century since her death, her writings have been neglected. Only students of Rilke and Nietzsche have been interested in her. It is worth a little reflection here to consider whether she has anything to offer the student of psychoanalysis—anything beyond the history of an exceptional personality. Is she to be thought of as one of our teachers, if a minor one, or only as one of our hypothetical patients?

I doubt very much that in the long run Lou Andreas-Salomé will turn out to have indicated the course which our theory ought to follow. Yet even this must be stated with qualifications. On the subject of female sexuality, we might listen attentively (or perhaps skeptically) to a woman who came to psychoanalysis from an already stated attitude toward the sexual life and did not alter her formulation of it greatly in consequence. Freudian theory is weak in its analysis of what it means to be a woman; principally the nonmale, the psychologically castrated aspect is worked out in it, in addition to that which is neither male nor female but generally human. The culturalist school has not helped the situation much by locating the cause of woman's feeling of inferiority and deprivation in the peculiarities of the social structure. Lou Andreas-Salomé boldly asserted femininity as a positive existence. She plainly exaggerated it, and there is a

marked reactive element in her position, influenced not only by
her personal life but also by the prevailing climate of feminism,
although it is also clear that she was not a feminist at all in the
usual sense. But the mother-goddess of the Stone Age has a vestigial descendant in Lou's ideal of womanhood, and we might
usefully keep her in mind.

The interpretation of religion in Lou Andreas-Salomé's writings is a sophisticated one, and for all her sharing in the convinced
agnosticism of her age, she drew on first-hand experience. She
agreed with Freud that religion was primitive and infantile, but
that was not where she saw its defect: the trouble lay rather in
the encounter of the religious spirit, erupting spontaneously from
man's fear and delight in his existence, with the cool reflection of mature rationality. The result has been sheer loss, in the
highly complex metaphysical religion of modern man, for her an
essentially devitalized spirituality. In the short paper "Jesus the
Jew," written in 1896 long before Freud's influence on her, she
anticipated finely the mental process whereby the image of the
god returns to its human creator and carries on its own life as the
ego ideal, to use Freud's later term. Elsewhere she suggests poeti-
cally a solution for the difficult technical question of religious differences between analyst and patient:

> The more openly the two proceed in their cooperative work
> toward the goal of health the more certainly they stand on com-
> mon ground, and the meaning of the question vanishes. In the
> harshness and barrenness of life's wanderings, however far they
> move in diverse directions, they quench their thirst from the
> same well, like the animals of the desert that meet at the same
> oasis at dawn and at the fall of evening.[27]

Despite the frequent obscurity of her thought, it is in such personal touches, intuitive certainly, but never abstracted from life,
that we gain illumination from her. Her own urge toward synthesis, toward a philosophical totality, failed. She was not a major theoretician, not a systematic thinker in psychoanalysis at all.

She recognized in psychoanalysis a unique contribution to human experience—a path to a world which has the stuff of poetry in it —and an infinity of surprise.

I

In Freud's School

GÖTTINGEN, SEPTEMBER 27, 1912

Lou Andreas-Salomé to Sigmund Freud

Ever since I was permitted to attend the Weimar Congress[28] last autumn, the study of psychoanalysis has had a constant hold on me. The deeper I get into it, the more it grips me. My wish to spend a few months in Vienna is now about to be fulfilled. Would you permit me to attend your classes and to be admitted to the Wednesday evening meetings? The sole purpose of my sojourn there is to devote myself to all phases of this subject.

VIENNA, OCTOBER 1, 1912

Sigmund Freud to Lou Andreas-Salomé

If you come to Vienna we shall all endeavor to make available to you the little there is in psychoanalysis that can be demonstrated and shared. Of course I have already looked on your participation at the Weimar Congress as a favorable omen.

OCTOBER 26, 1912

Beginning of Classes

On the twenty-fifth, as Ellen[29] and I stood by the window of the train approaching Vienna, we had the thought: everything is already fully determined in all its interconnections; that is, everything that is to befall us is already here. Some amusing incidents have occurred. At the very start of my quest for a *pension* I ran into Dr. Jekels.[30] He informed me that Freud's class was about to begin today. Freud's house, where I am to go for an admission card, turns out to be close by. The auditorium of the psychiatric clinic, which I expected to find at the university, is practically in front of our Hotel Zita. And only a few steps farther to the *Alte Elster* restaurant, where the Freud group gathers after the lecture and at other times. A promising beginning.

Freud looks older and more harassed than in the days of the Weimar Congress; he talked about that too while we walked part way home together. Maybe it's the fight with Stekel,[31] which is now in full swing. The lecture might have been a deliberate attempt to scare us away, with all the difficulties of psychoanalysis: even if we should succeed in wresting something from the unconscious, "swiftly, as a diver snatches something from the abyss," any generalization derived from this bit would be promptly turned into a caricature. Since we have access to the unconscious only through pathological material, our efforts arouse the resistance of the conscious, awake individual.

Yet all this is inconsequential compared with the one great fact which he did *not* mention: that it is of the essence of his simple and ingenious approach to make something unconscious comprehensible by grasping it in illness and kindred states. Only through pathological material could sure knowledge be won, only there where the inner life makes a detour and betrays a little of itself, is formulated through expression, and can be caught with the logical hook in the shallows that shift between the surface and the depths. I recalled how this thought took hold of me on my first acquaintance with Freud's ideas, when I happened on them for the first time in passing in Swoboda's[32] writings. Swoboda's concept of the unconscious is to Freud's as the living germ, growing and maturing, is to the bygone, sterilized product; but for that very reason Swoboda could never offer any evidence without recourse to metaphysics, and his "periodicity" is only a half-hearted attempt to draw the subject into the sphere of scientific observation. Consequently while it can be integrated with Freud's assumptions, when for example, concrete data are involved, even then it has nothing profound to say about their origins. But just when Swoboda does say something of the sort he falls into philosophical speculation, which Freud can avoid completely by remaining in the realm of empirical interpretation, bringing to light something really new.

That is where the emphasis must always be placed.

VIENNA, AUGUST 6, 1912

Alfred Adler[33] *to Lou Andreas-Salomé*

Your letter, and the prospect of seeing you in Vienna in October, are so closely associated in my mind that I thank you for both at the same time. I share your appreciation of Freud's scientific significance up to the point at which I further and further parted company with him. His heuristic model is certainly important and useful as such, since it contains in reflection all the features of a psychic system *as well*. But in addition to that, Freud's school has taken sexual phraseology for the heart of the matter. It may be that Freud the man has provoked a critical attitude in me. I cannot regret it.

OCTOBER 28, 1912

Visit to Alfred Adler

First visit to Alfred Adler. Until late at night. He is charming and very intelligent. Only a couple of things bothered me. First, that he spoke of the prevailing controversies in far too personal a manner. Second, that he looks like a button. As though he had gotten stuck somewhere inside himself. I told him that I had not actually come to him from my study of psychoanalysis, but from work in the psychology of religion, which finds ample confirmation in his book *The Neurotic Constitution*,[34] and which touches on related ideas connected with the formation of fictions. But in point of fact we never got very far. Not even when we got into a rather lively dispute over psychoanalysis during supper. I considered it unproductive that, in order for him to cling to the terms "above" and "below" and "masculine protest," the "feminine" must always have a negative sign, while passivity as such, functioning sexually or generally, is a *positive* foundation of ego function. Accordingly he deprives submission of any real, positive quality, simply because he designates it "a feminine means to masculine goals"; which, however, is promptly avenged in the theory of neurosis, since the concept of compromise is consequently impossible. Freud on the contrary, even in the past when he attributed the neuroses to exclusively sexual determinants, always recognized compromise as essential, that is, the mutual interference of two components. Adler achieves a merely specious solution through his secondary safeguards which are directly antithetical to overcompensations of inferiority feelings through the agency of primary safeguards; in the secondary safeguards the repressed instinctual life breaks out masked, only to be considered as yet another contrivance of the psyche.

To me every neurosis appears to be a mutual conflict between ego and sexuality. Instead of promoting each other, they abuse each other, the ego being constricted by sexual tendencies, sexuality by the ego tendencies. The ego instinct, for example, is sexualized in cruelty (sadism), and the sexual, in masochism, bursts the bounds of the ego into the latter's territory.

I found what Adler had to say about Stekel most uncongenial, including his private designs on Stekel's journal, this despite the fact that he knew perfectly well how Stekel had earned it. All the same he took Stekel to be a good fellow, certainly not essentially bad, but on the other hand without the intellectual qualities to be able to *penetrate* deeply. What I liked best in Adler was the mobility of his mind, whereby many divergent things could be woven together; the trouble is that it is superficial and unreliable, *skipping* about when it should pace off the distances. Thus Adler now makes everything sexual ego symbol that until recently had been sexual symbol disguised as ego; this goes far beyond Freud, who admitted an organic rather than a psychosexual function.

On the way home, Adler invited me to his Thursday evening conferences. I shall speak frankly about it with Freud. I accepted with pleasure.

OCTOBER 29, 1912

Alfred Adler to Lou Andreas-Salomé

I should be most obliged if you would not discuss with anyone our conversation on the subject of Stekel and Freud's *Zentralblatt*. Your silence can hurt no one and will keep me from being drawn into the fight that has flared up between Stekel and Freud. Believe me, I do not want to take a stand on either side.

The Nature of Punishment

My wide window looks out on the garden, from where only the twittering of the autumn birds comes to awaken me in the morning. The room might have been designed for work, but I have not yet gotten to it. Read the current issue of *Imago*[35] today, in which Freud has published the best of his papers on savages and neurotics. I find the idea most appealing that moral misconduct, quite like scientific fact in our sense of the word today, was once considered to actually affect the entire cosmos. Hence if there was no immediate evidence of punishment, people took it on themselves in self-protection, rather like the way in which infected persons are isolated and infected things are burned. Freud here detects the origin of punishment, and I myself think that this motive is, next to the urge for vengeance, largely operative in the blood feud. Maybe for the same reason too, the blood avenger might be adopted after the deed as a child into the family and permitted to kiss the breasts of the mother. And further, our emphasis on the motive rather than the act, the so-called higher ethical evaluation only seemingly raises the ethical level; as a matter of fact, it grows out of the shrinking of the cosmos, once of unimaginable sanctity and now of practical necessity looked on only matter-of-factly. Now at all events, it is human nobility that is underscored. Yet while that reaches more and more into all the sophistries of morality, the tie with life's real ground slackens at the same time, so that in the end nothing remains but hygiene, the stepchild of morality. What primitive man knew all along, that life is all we have to obey, that "joy is perfection" (Spinoza), *we* rediscover only in states of untrammeled ecstasy antithetical to morality—inspired states of the noblest egoism.

OCTOBER 30, 1912

Wednesday Discussion: Nature of Neurosis—Adler's View

Came very early. Only one man was already there, a blond fellow with a big head, Dr. Tausk.[36] Conversation about Buber.[37] I found myself in disagreement with something Tausk said, but I forgot it right away and never got to talk to him about it.

Freud seated me at his side and made a very sweet remark. He gave the paper. During the discussion we talked quietly together on various matters. I was surprised how readily he acquiesced to a view of neurosis as a conflict between libido and ego instead of proceeding unilaterally from the libido. When I commented that it read otherwise in his books he said, "My latest formulation." And that corresponds with my general impression: that the theory is by no means hidebound, but is adjusted to further findings, and, further, that this man is great simply in that he is the man of research advancing quietly and working tirelessly. Perhaps the "dogmatism" with which he is reproached derives from the necessity to establish guidelines in the course of his tireless advance, if only for the sake of his fellow-workers.

Had a discussion with him and Dr. Federn[38] during the intermission, Federn defending Adler's theory of inferiority as applied to children. I supported Freud's ideas: it is the strength of the child, his feeling of superiority in fact, that he wants everything because he has a claim on everything, not because he compensates in that way for a feeling of inferiority. His claims and his deprivations do not yet give rise to any schism. It is only the neurotically disposed child that makes the supposed claim for compensation, often without having endured any social rebuff. It is still an open question whether the neurotically disposed child must be organically inferior, which Adler holds and which Freud denies—pointing to the extremely frail and yet happily secure child, on the one hand, and the equally common "healthy" neurotic one, on the other. Naturally any psychic illness is also a physical illness, the sole question being whether it lies within the realm of what we can grasp and define as organic illness. Maybe Adler's contention holds only with respect to the truism that in the last analysis psychic and physical are identical, while it falls in its principal implication that specific psychic events are based on specific organic defects. He tries thus to supply neurotic processes allegedly in full consciousness with a foundation from below instead of falling back on the Freudian mechanisms of the unconscious. His book on *Organ Inferiority*,[39] which was not yet committed to these corollaries of his theory, was of extraordinary interest to me.

After this I just cannot go to *his* evening discussion tomorrow, and I told him so by telephone.

NOVEMBER 2, 1912

Lecture: Ucs.—Complex—Instinct

Again by way of introduction; this time on the concept of the unconscious (Ucs.) considered by him from three aspects (descriptive, dynamic, systematic). It is new for me to hear from Freud's mouth the proposition that the material of the unconscious need not necessarily consist only of the repressed, but also of that which has barely reached the vicinity of consciousness, only, so to speak, to be turned away at the door. This concession might have wide-ranging significance.

The present fights have the fascinating effect that Freud sets forth his views about the dissensions on different occasions. This time expressly about Jung's defection.[40] He showed a subtle and ingenious bit of malice in his attempt to make the term "complex" superfluous, pointing out how it had insinuated itself into the terminology out of convenience, without having grown up on psychoanalytic soil, just as Dionysus was artificially exalted from being an exotic god to becoming the son of Zeus. (At this, Tausk, who was sitting or standing next to Freud, and was still in the white doctor's smock he wore coming from the psychiatric clinic, did not quite stifle a chuckle.)

The concept of complexes, he went on to say, ought to pertain to the substantial content (as the Zürich school discovered on the basis of associative reactions to stimulus words) but that explains nothing about the mode of effect or of liability to illness —since everyone has a father–mother complex and so forth. Freud did not mention here how nicely the word does fit his notion of the power of certain unconscious facts to suck or draw to themselves whatever is analogous to them and how nicely it therefore fills a mediate position between illness and health. Everyone does have complexes, but their inordinate strength implies, if not illness, then certainly the disposition to it, since they exert their attractive powers so ominously, and compete with conscious elaboration.

Apropos of the concept of instinct, Freud made use of the customary definition that it "rests on the organic." As long as the instinct theory remains just that which physiologists and psychologists toss at one another—no further enlightenment can emerge from it, even with Freud. It also remains as a mere crutch, an unwilled inconsistency in our knowledge of nature and of mind. Perhaps it can be attributed to this predicament that Adler ultimately could classify the instinctual life among the other symbolic forms of his "psychic rules of the game." For if "instinct" is only, so to speak, a limiting concept viewed from two aspects, then a specific property can be attributed to it only by means of a bilateral optical illusion.

Once again, however, it is a mark of greatness in Freud how, untroubled by such philosophic worries, he merely proceeds to action on such questions. So he was able to sketch out a map of a whole country on the basis of this border region, before anyone even knew whose land he was entering, with the sole aid of a few straggling trespassers driven by necessity to disregard the border regulations. In mental illness he grabbed hold of life by the coat-tails, just there where it appears to us squeezed helplessly into a cleft, unable to escape into the organic alone (the organic into which everything escapes and becomes "physical," when we are unable to understand it in psychological terms), and there he put it to the question. Indeed Freud's great discovery cannot be better described than by saying that he made a virtue for science out of the necessity of mental life. There where the psychical picture distorted by illness beyond its normal contours threatened to fall out of the framework of comprehensibility, Freud succeeded in approaching it from *both* sides: not only from the side of the elusive vital processes which will not in the normal state present themselves to science, but also from the other side, of analysis into individual components, which hitherto were known only as a phenomenon of physical disintegration. It is therefore surely no accident that it was a physician who stood this egg of Columbus on its head and found that it would stand upright on its broken end.

NOVEMBER 4, 1912

Sigmund Freud to Lou Andreas-Salomé

Since you have informed me of your plan to attend Adler's evening group I am taking the liberty, unasked, to say a few words to you by way of orientation in this disagreeable state of affairs. The kind of relations which ought to obtain between two analogous although divergent enterprises simply does not exist between these two groups. Something quite different from psychoanalysis is often being practiced alongside of it. We have been forced to stop all intercourse between Adler's splinter group and our own association, and our medical guests are also requested to choose which of the two they will visit. That is unpleasant, but the personal behavior of the defectors leaves us no choice.

It is not my purpose, my dear lady, to enforce such limitations in your case. I only request of you that with due regard for the situation you make use of an artificial psychic split, so to speak, and make no mention there of your role here and vice versa.

NOVEMBER 6, 1912

Wednesday Discussion: Sadomasochism

Freud's official account of Stekel's withdrawal (as if it concerned the local Vienna society only—whereas I know from Adler what Stekel's intentions are, and Freud also now recognizes them. But on this I had to be silent). Sadger's[41] lecture on sadomasochism. Freud had not much to say by way of concluding remarks, and he excused us all for being bored. He rightly supposed that if disgust with the topic did not itself create resistances, objective interest would have waned anyhow since the material, disgusting as it was, was also not meaningfully organized. But there is something about Sadger giving one the impression that it is not so much ability that he lacks as the desire to elevate the material through intellectual penetration from the unattractiveness of its crude content—as if in fact the demands of analysis disturbed his blissful contemplation. He presumably enjoys his analysands more than he helps them or learns anything from them.

Conversation with Freud about his sweet letter which I shall cherish as a present.

Home with Tausk and Federn, talking about Adler to whom

Federn I suspect does more justice than Tausk, but Adler would get more from the latter's adherence. Tausk intends to offer a course on Freud which I shall be happy to attend.

In Adler's Circle

When I arrived at Adler's today, he was in the midst of a telephone conversation with Stekel, all of which I heard (on Stekel's impending "secession" from Freud). Conversing with Adler I was much enlightened by the history of his development as a student of Marx, primarily interested in economics and philosophic speculation. Just as with the proletariat, social utopianism is supported on the basis of envy and hate, so, in Adler's view of the child, the exalted utopian ideal of personality arises on the basis of social comparison. Hence his rationalistic milieu therapy—and between it and the doctrine of organ inferiority based on physiology, the Freudian Ucs. falls to the ground—as it were between bodily defects and the formation of ideals. Hence Adler is accorded the approval of both physiologists and theoretical psychologists more readily than Freud is, but he has sacrificed the fundamental issue and that is why his solution is no salvation—which will no doubt become evident in *practice*.

Inasmuch as he believes that the sole basis of inferiority is physical and that physical inferiority is based on the genital, he represents his differences with Freud too drastically, since whenever bodily infirmity from another source is not present to explain matters, he expresses the *libido theory* in the form of "organ dialect."

With Adler during Oppenheim's[42] lecture on Faust, Part II, second lecture. Good and interesting. Furtmüller[43] also led a stimulating discussion (of Faust as the example of inferiority in quest of compensation, to be satisfied only by the unattainable); but it was readily clear that the distinguishing boundary between creativity and neurosis was obliterated and with it the problem. Adler's group could be very stimulating if only he stayed *outside* psychoanalysis.

C. G. Jung: Libido

Read his latest and fateful work; [44] Tausk brought me the *Jahrbuch* to read during a day spent at the hotel. Unhappily I had to miss Freud's seminar, Harden [45] having insisted on my seeing him.

In the course of my racing through Jung's opus it seemed to me that his main error is the same as Adler's, a premature and hence quite sterile synthesis. But Adler is not taken in by developmental theory and the nonsense about monism and energetics, and he proceeds more philosophically, i.e., from the fact of consciousness itself. Jung does the opposite: he tries to explain the libido, and, in order to make the concept all-inclusive, he attenuates it correspondingly, in both directions. Thus he prefixes a *pre*sexual stage of the libido to which ego instincts like hunger appertain and which is sublimated *post*sexually into all spiritual potentials. This sort of naïve philosophizing is the strongest evidence that the true monist, while employing unifying concepts, can still tolerate dualism, i.e., the manifest polarity of all phenomena, on empirical grounds and not strip the life out of it in order to arrive at a barren and subjective system. I liked Jung's account of the incest concept and his amplification of it to the idea of "longing for the mother's womb." In general sexual symbolism could still receive its due—provided that he does not emphasize it only at the expense of the prohibited term "incest." One is sometimes led to suspect that a quarrel over terms results when the real issue is much deeper and not a terminological one at all.

NOVEMBER 10, 1912

Sigmund Freud to Lou Andreas-Salomé

If I understand you rightly, you would like a personal exchange of ideas. I should myself have proposed it definitely a long time ago, if the business of founding the new psychoanalytic journal had not added to my usual activities.

I do not know whether a discussion after ten o'clock at night conforms with your daily routine, but I have no free time earlier than that. If you will do me the honor of a visit at such a late hour, I shall gladly engage to see you safely home. Wednesday evening then, we can decide on the day.

I missed you yesterday at the lecture, and I am happy to hear that your absence was not occasioned by a visit to the camp of the masculine protest. I have acquired the bad habit of directing my lecture to a particular person in the audience, and yesterday I stared as if spellbound at the vacant chair reserved for you.

NOVEMBER 12, 1912

Adler's Address to the Medical Society

Ellen and I went together and laughed a lot at all the goings on. Later went again with Adler and some others to a café where Adler was amusing and amiable. Serious conversation with him only *en route*. But he just can not be pinned down. So with reference to the analysis he presented in his address: expressions of pain could really be "arrangement," yet they also seemed to have plenty of other causes. By his account any such manifestations even in animals may indicate "arrangement" and the demand for attention. Now such a pallid generalization says nothing—as little, for example, as his other pronouncement that all physically ill persons are neurotics and vice versa. For in both instances you have to make new distinctions and classifications in order to reach positive insights starting from these vague commonplaces. The upshot of it is only the illusion of knowing something more than before. Another point is the uncertainty of the neurotic who expects everything of the future, experiences the present anxiously, and for whom misery remains misery even when it is compensated. In contrast to the construction of fictions for the purpose of compensation, the fictions of healthy people, by anticipating the prospects of the future, bring them to life in the present; the future is inwardly present before it is disclosed externally. In such a sense, "primitive" man, too, in his primary religiousness was able to create his deities, in the confidence of being their descendant, while in animal strength he was himself in danger of succumbing to more powerful animals. Diametrically opposed to this inwardly operative presence of the spiritual future stands the postponement of the whole present into the future, the external, the beyond, the time to come, which characterizes customary religion. The two kinds of faith are as sharply and precisely distinguished as creative processes are from neurotic. But Adler's "as if" confuses them.

NOVEMBER 13, 1912

Wednesday Discussion: an Analysis

Sadger's protracted second lecture on sadomasochism was mitigated by Freud's summary of an analysis.

A "highspirited" woman, who required masochistic satisfaction from her partner to remain faithful: forcible spreading of her legs, being examined, insulted, and so forth, to which she added the fantasy that other observers were present. It was not for this reason, however, that she came to Freud, but on account of attacks of vertigo which threatened to deprive her of her livelihood, at a time when she still had to support her old father—producing anxiety partly on that account, partly on account of her secret wishes to be freed of her financial burden by the death of her father. But the attacks of vertigo arose out of her identification with him. He, too, suffered from them and hence was her libidinal model, he too was given to insults whilst her mother behaved more decently. She had been examined by the doctor in childhood for her enuresis. (Did this recollection enable her to exaggerate the verbal masochism to a fantasy of something deadly, linked with sexuality?) As the analysis unearthed the father-complex, her father on one occasion appeared among the *observers* in the recovered memory of the examination. Thereupon the whole performance became transparent and consequentially impossible. To her sorrow she was cured of it, along with her attacks of vertigo and with it the possibility of her remaining faithful.

Home with Tausk and Federn, who then repaired to the Ronacher Café. Spoke about Freud. Tausk at such times speaks passionately. A lot of it fits my external picture of Freud, especially, for example, as he enters the class with the appearance of moving to the side. There is in this gesture a will to solitude, a concealment of himself within his own purposes, which by his preference would be no concern of his school or his public. And especially when you look above the gesture to the brow and the glance, so calm, so wise and strong.

Lecture: Dream Symbols

In the small auditorium, which I found only because Rank[46] and Sadger were likewise wandering around lost.

On dream symbols. Their distinction from the mere pictorial element in dreams, which is perfectly capable of being deciphered simultaneously by the associations of the patient. A symbol can be definitely counted on as such (1) where it recurs constantly, (2) when it intervenes appropriately when associations cease, (3) when connections are clarified thereby, (4) and (5) when it appears to be well founded in idiom and etymology. Usually only a few of these conditions are fulfilled, so that the interpretation is left to intuition, a nonscientific procedure, although often productive. An inconsiderable number of symbols are as yet confirmed, and these are practically all of sexual origin.

It can be added that symbolic images of a sexual nature must of necessity become typical for nearly everything partly because they represent images from antiquity, when the physical and mental had not yet been strictly differentiated; partly because they constantly arise in us anew from levels in which sexuality and the ego are still profoundly interpenetrating; and finally and particularly because the pictorial quality of the physical assures it of being preferentially grasped as symbol. In dream as in delusion, the symbol may be frequently misinterpreted with respect to its content, while its form could be used (and it might sometimes be misunderstood by the dreamer or the neurotic himself). But I think this point of view needs to be considered not only with respect to images but also to the seemingly undisguised and formless content itself. Many a bloody scene of incest, many a crime black as night, or perversity shimmering in a spectrum of color in dreams and in delusions springs from depths reaching to

the impenetrable core of narcissism and can only most inadequately be included in such terms. I do not mean to say that the
crudity of the language ought to be modified. On the contrary, it
is good as it is, certainly for the time being, and it keeps us from
resorting once more to our old rose-colored spectacles and from
making concessions of principle to middlemen under the guise
of terminological refinement. Meanwhile, however, if we take the
terms too literally in individual cases and forget that *alles Vergängliche*[47] is only an image, it could happen that instead of
showing the patient a true picture of himself, we might ourselves
be taken in by the very picture which his neurosis has portrayed
with all its horrible exaggerations, anchored as they are in the
mute ocean of inner experience that can be depicted only in the
caricatures of an almost monstrous mythology of the soul.

Freud used the expression "archaic" a few times, with reference to the child's way of thinking: that is, the child thinks ar-
chaically in his ignorance of sex distinctions. He ought to have
said "infantile." For surely primitive people, and animals too, distinguish sharply between the sexes, in contrast to the youngster
for whom the genital sphere does not yet exist.

Technique of Dream and Waking— Poetic Technique

Precisely as dreams in accord with their latent content are
rationalized into manifest forms which we are able to recall, so
our waking also proceeds. Only, from our waking point of view,
we ignore and devaluate still more thoroughly the latent contribution—if indeed we take thought of it at all during the day-
time. But in reality no one quite grasps the feeling that his
life is lived as if behind a curtain, behind all the conscious events
of waking existence. If we are inclined to doubt the truthfulness
of journals and memoirs, it is not just on account of their

conscious or half-conscious omissions. Above all it is because the construction of memoirs, like narrated dreams, amounts to a rationalization of experience, *eo ipso* a falsification of its latent essence. If a person thinks back over the entire course of his life, he is struck by the discontinuity and poor selectivity of the points that stand out clearly in his memory. Transitions and bridges of logical reflection must do their best to provide the connections. Many "unforgettable" events are strikingly banal, indifferent, or meaningless, while incidents which have claimed our deepest interest have to our sorrow become unintelligible in their precious details. Here too, by means of the associative process, significant latent content may very likely evolve out of the fragments, exactly as with the dream; the picture which emerges in all these lines, broken at the surface but pressing vertically into the depths, is a picture quite different from the horizontal structure of our waking memory.

So, too, a *literary* technique could be imagined (that old dream of mine!) which would be true to that very unity of formation. It would concentrate its poetic creativity on just this, instead of on spatiotemporal representation—which we all feel ought to be *non-*literary, i.e., it ought to be simple and true like factual information. On such grounds the latter approach to writing keeps any mature person away from epic productions of otherwise greater literary quality and turns him instead to the intensively detailed psychological analysis of the modern novel, in the correct expectation that the picture can be validly completed only psychologically. The analysis, however, deals abstractly and unpoetically with the colorful living form and loses the *unity* of the images through their isolation. Instead, it should restrict itself to that which can be really suggested only through the agency of poetry, namely that unity which psychoanalysis constructs piecemeal; of it Freud remarked once that to bring about the construction of the completed analysis in reverse from the end to the beginning would require an artist. The supremely individual stays back by itself away from the typical, in which, in its special form, everything is once more recognized and so the great elemental themes recur, which children love and legends created. Yes, the fairy tale itself, the descendant of the legend, would become genuine and possible again, not "imitation." (MARGINAL NOTE: Poetry is something between the dream and its interpretation.)

Awakening from dreams, one often retains, quite independently of the present content of the dream, the feeling as of a merry dance. Then one feels more clearly that the essential unity of the state of mind lies far behind the dream fragments. The dream is split up and made manifold to oblige the rationalizing process. Conversely with waking, or the waking state in the logical sense: *its* very reality lies in the *cleavage* between the ego and that which confronts the ego. The faculty of having an inner experience tends toward *unification*. When we are awake we hold to be unreal whatever is purely subjective and is found to be unrelated to the external world; for the external world is of its substance and can be separated only by artifice. The unreal in the dream therefore is just what emerges from subjectivity into all the manifold dream realities. In this way the dream tends to reach out of the fundamental reality of the unconscious which unites both subject and object.

Just because the dream does have this tendency, it possesses a touch of the pathological element that is characteristic of neurosis and even psychosis. As far as the waking state, on the contrary, tends toward reunification, *its* reality is also rooted in unconscious reality; *en route*, however, in every moment of life, waking life is split and hence in principle it, too, resembles illness, except for the fact that it more successfully approaches its aim. From the first stirrings of the dream all the way to full consciousness we are only *en route*.

NOVEMBER 19, 1912

Tausk's Course in Psychoanalysis

Swoboda visited me in the afternoon; in the evening I went to Tausk's course, having missed the first session of it to go to Adler's.

I have by now frequently talked with Tausk, always with pleasure, but without getting to know him very well. My clearest impression of him came from his remarks during the discussion of Sadger's paper (on sadomasochism); they were so congenial to me that I might have made them myself.

Actually I never make any remarks at all, unless I just can not restrain myself, and then Freud takes them up in the discussion.

Tausk's way of lecturing, proceeding from the periphery to the center, the opposite order from the way that Freud's teachings have come about, is a first-rate way to make them quite naturally plausible. Many terms seemed to me to be introduced too early ("narcissism"—that most difficult of all). In other places I thought it possible that an occasional malicious reference to Adler might do harm to Tausk himself, and unfairly, for he emphasizes the ego instinct alongside the sexual motivation and stresses the difference between the typical and the individual. In fact one gets the impression not only of classical Freudian theory but also of an unusually loving and reverent approach to the essential discoveries of Freud—discoveries like "condensation," "displacement," and so forth, so valuable in themselves beyond all theory 'and like those excavated objects of antiquity possessing in themselves a value not lessened by their being only torsos.

A thin green-eyed student opened a good discussion. (On whether we repress on account of the stress of unpleasure or whether we *want* to repress for that reason. Perhaps his principal contention might be conceded, namely that "we consciously want" it, insofar as the repressed idea had already *been* conscious.)

Wednesday Discussion: Freud on Swoboda

Reports. Ferenczi[48] in from Budapest; by way of introduction he explained his plans concerning the editorship taken over in place of Stekel. His manner was objective and likable. I feel altogether more at home and more comfortable every time I am with all these people around Freud. Whether that is his doing or the result of the work, it is good to be here.

Interesting drawing of a room by a neurotic patient; Federn passed it around. Trifling objects in the room recalled earlier, more important ones later and harder to recall, until finally bare places on the wall represent a complete absence of ideas, but in the end the most significant thing leads back to the earliest associations (blue lampshade, "blue misery," Madonna with the blue vault of heaven over the globe). Freud spoke a lot and spiritedly on the occasion of Rosenstein's[49] exposition of Swoboda's work. Freud said exactly what I myself had observed last year about him and Swoboda: the latter speaks exclusively of the manifest content of the dream, and this does away with the contradictions between the two theories, but also makes less significant the "periodic" dream interpretations and the confirmation of the twenty-eight- and twenty-three-day periods in dreams.

In Adler's Circle: Homosexuality—Stekel

Furtmüller held that Freud "resorted to single facts as ultimates, while Adler reduced even these to psychic fictions." That is not so, however; to closer observation the facts ultimately vanish for Adler only in that he hides epistemologically behind the illusoriness of events, the "as if." Since it is not this that counts, but the practical orientation, it is again necessary to make distinctions and separations within the illusoriness of such events, i.e., to again establish the categories of the "psychic" and the "real." There Freud once more would come in with his challenge: to pursue the psychic as far as possible with psychic means, that is, up to the point where only somatic signs are left to us. These are sexually determined, and in them we are, as it were, involved in the totality beyond the ego. Whatever game the psyche may play with them, from this standpoint it can go no further, since there would be no bridges between the pysche and purely somatic "organ feeling."

I felt strengthened in my opinion by the lecture on homosexuality that followed, by Adler himself (primarily a case history). The homosexual whom he portrayed is basically not that at all; he does not construct his homosexual fiction out of the real facts of life, but on the contrary he is alienated from reality and shuns the facts exactly as a neurotic likes to do. He is not neurotic in that he is homosexual, but he is homosexual in that he is neurotic and needs precisely this fiction. An instinctually organized homosexual will perhaps even construct a quite different, contrary fiction in opposition to his real desire in order to protect himself against it. And only in so-called normal persons do the real elements and the psychic intentions cooperatively form the integrated personality. Stekel appeared in the group and was frequently quoted in the papers. Although I sat at an adjacent table with Ellen this time, he came over and interrogated me about Freud; we became rather embroiled. As I could not make a scene about it, being Adler's guest, Ellen and I left during the intermission. But Stekel came too. He had to deny that he adhered to the Adlerian views we had just heard, and this on the street and with all manner of witnesses.

Quite apart from his presence there, in the present state of affairs it is plain that I shall have to drop out of Adler's evening discussions. They are interesting to be sure, but interest is not what I am after.

Physical and Psychical

Adler's concept of the "somatic foundations of neuroses": naturally they do exist, but no one knows anything about them. Where our entire inner experience is at our disposal, we know very little about its bodily equivalents; and conversely, where physical processes are visibly apparent to us, or else can be easily extrapolated, the psychic accompaniment of these processes is not accessible. The heart of the matter is, I think, fundamentally philosophical (and that is why the famous "parallelism" is not fully realizable). That is, we understand as "physical" just that which is not psychically accessible, that which we do not feel to be identical with our own ego in itself, and hence that which we place at a distance from the ego, i.e., as distinct from the mental. It is intrinsically one and the same thing to say "not explicable in mental terms," "necessitating a physical explanation," and hence "material." It is self-explanatory, therefore, that the bodily processes equivalent to mental processes are hidden from us. We cannot do otherwise than investigate each domain with the appropriate method as far as possible, since, methodologically speaking, everything is comprised in each of them. At no time and in no place is one to be related to the other as cause to effect; only the eye of God would contemplate their unity; and only for the philosopher, never for the empiricist, is the unity manifest, in Spinoza's sense.

In those places, however, where the two methods and the two worlds stand closest to one another, where we cease to interpret in "mental" terms, and where we must begin to do so "physically," there, as it were, with a bad conscience, uncertainty, and ambiguity, we speak of processes in the brain and nervous system or of endocrine relationships. When disturbance or illness is disclosed we once more are promptly made aware of such an interaction of "body" and "mind"; we are made to feel mental sufferings in a physical way and endure physical disorder mentally. Hence it comes to pass that a seemingly psychogenic illness is medically accessible and a physically "determined" one yields to psychic influences. (Thus internists confirm the presence of toxic substances in the blood in bronchial asthma, without objecting to psychological treatment. Conversely: the nasal cautery against masturbation, and so on.[50])

Is it not striking that those very bodily agencies which we consider to be most closely associated with the expressions of mental activity—brain, spinal cord (the nervous substance)—appear the least differentiated? They are made up of pulpy masses protectively enclosed by a bony capsule or a thin little cord without any special distinguishing characteristics visible to us. On the other hand, there is the infinitely miraculous world of "mindless" nature of myriad forms, from which our senses and our thought never cease to learn. (Another objection to the occultists, that when they "materialize" psychic stuff, they just for that reason bring nothing psychic to us, *and not even as much as matter.*)

We can bring the psychic closest to our understanding only by more-or-less personifying it in physical form, and we grasp the psychic only in the images of the external world. We make use of the inorganic world in spiritual symbols, and we have to illustrate spiritual events with the help of fundamental material processes that are equally incomprehensible.

NOVEMBER 26, 1912

Tausk's Course: Sex and Ego

The green-eyed student was once more very keen in the discussion. He noted correctly that forgetting through repression is still a purely mechanical process while the "substitute" idea already seems to presuppose an intention. Although Tausk looks so remarkably wretched, he carries the banner of leadership well. In many of his observations during the discussion I found him *too* precisely Freudian; in any case, he is never likely to be reproached with the contrary.

In most of Freud's writing, civilized man appears as a sadly domesticated savage, and his sublimation by the aid of his repressed savagery assumes an essentially negative quality—drive and culture being contrasted like the inner and outer value. According to Freud that seems to be a corollary of the concept of narcissism, which, to be sure, includes the sexual and the ego instincts without distinction, but in such a way that ultimately every function of the ego appears essentially hostile to sexuality. Hence the end of all culture appears as a constant attenuation of the instincts, a frightful transfiguration! In actuality, however, health really means their mutual adjustment, neurosis their mutual discord; the ego, which is manifest in culture, must find in it directly the forms in which it will fully discharge its instinctual energy. For culture does not only confront the ego; it also expresses its own individually elaborated development at the same time (analogously with the repression of the erogenous zones in physical development; regardless of whether this came to be on account of external prohibitions, it works to the benefit of the genital, since it results in the concentration of pleasurable stimuli in that zone). That which constitutes narcissism and which undoubtedly accompanies us all our lives in a mysterious way must also come again and again to be the *creative* element, i.e., the natural and at the same time the spiritual goal of every human development, the *unity* of sex and ego.

Wednesday Discussion: Narcissism, Methodology

Tausk's lecture on inhibitions of artists. I recall a few observations on two analyses which he presented—of a writer and a painter—and much of what he said seemed very good, but the rest is gone, not having been noted down. On narcissism ("in which we are at one with our desires"): how every renewal of life, following neuroses and also in creativity, again and again springs from it; that the neuroses of artists—maybe for that reason—while especially common, are of lesser magnitude than those of uncreative people. Lastly the relation between narcissism and anal erotism (in which we conceive of our own work, something which has become objectified, as if it were our own self). Thence to the father-complex and so forth.

Freud's rejoinders were more severe than usual and yet no other person presents his papers to him with such evident reverence. I think that Tausk is of all the most unconditionally devoted to Freud and at the same time the most prominently outstanding.

Freud's replies emphasized: (1) That the difficulties with material grasped so recently are too great to treat them in a polished lecture; the number of original, synthesizing ideas deserve recognition, but the crying need is for greater depth in the details of the research.

(2) That with the persistent calumny of our whole movement on the part of official science, we should not dare to move so

boldly into new territory leaving the rear so exposed, and confirmation of earlier discoveries needs to be made again and again. (This last indeed is the real reason why Freud had to organize a school and a following, instead of pursuing his lone researches by himself—a second reason for his conflict with independent, or temperamental, characters.)

(3) The obscurity which still prevails around the process and definition of sublimation; Tausk's "partial" sublimation might actually be less a threshold of sublimation than a necessary condition for success in artistic work. (Freud here appears wonderfully undogmatic vis-à-vis his own terminology and quite unhindered by it in his research.)

(4) How all therapy appears to find its limits at the narcissistic stage and at bottom can only move within already discharged libidinal cathexes; but an analysis *must* attempt to penetrate to this point.

Freud has returned almost too refreshed and content from the trip to Munich[51] on the matter of Stekel's journal. (It was on account of this trip that last Saturday's seminar was omitted.) Is the understanding with Jung really such a certainty as it officially sounded on Wednesday?

Since then we all are supposed to behave "diplomatically" on the Jung affair; but actually Munich was already a rupture.

NOVEMBER 30, 1912

Lecture: Wish Dream—Disgust and Sexuality

Freud commented why it is that the designation "wish dream" or wish-fulfillment dream must not be used to classify the contents of the dream (confessions, warnings, proposals, and so on) or, if so, only in the illogical fashion in which one speaks of "baby and stomach doctors." All the same, I believe that the word "wish-fulfillment" itself has an excessively heavy ring and frequently leads to confusion. It is too strong a word, like almost all Freud's terminology which is so unequivocally honest; the word "wish," blue with night and longing, is applied literally where we ought to understand instead the pellucid colorlessness of our primal being, freed from our waking thought and hence silently fulfilled in the dream.

When he spoke on "Defiance and Anal Erotism," he linked "the anal character as a result of the sexual" too superficially with the punishment applied to the anal region itself. That can be misunderstood. The most difficult problems are interrelated here as they are in anal erotism generally. The vivid language in this case provides grounds for the resentment which his investigations have encountered, as if people never got over the yellow-brown hue of the word. We are made of earth and derive from it the beginnings of character and of sexuality; but it is also earth which is the finest filter of what we call the most shameful filth—finer than any filter devised by man, and through it alone the purest springs are guided to us. It is interesting that the disgust appropriate and healthy in all of us—the only "healthy" and self-evident disgust, lies here at the real point of origin of the individual. (So according to Freud's impressive analysis of the Macduff legend,[52] anxiety in its first prototypical form lies in the birth process, in being born.) All neurotic disgust is only the magnified image of the primary disgust, and thus we find already in it the profoundly significant connection of the worthless and the most precious, the evil and bad with the best and the creative forces of humanity. There is little ethical or aesthetic contemplation that does not find its deepest roots here.

And it is also interesting that this first, inescapable disgust is absent from sexuality from the start. This is a problem in itself. For as disgust arises within anality, through its repression (by training) it is still something which manifestly belongs to natural development, but only human development. Here then is a prob-

lem. It is as if normal human sexuality matured only at this distance from excretion and the inorganic.

Male and Female

I have been to Swoboda's seminar a couple of times on his
invitation. It never gets beyond the substance of his writings,
which I already know well, and it is brilliant in the same way,
maybe too much so. The will to brilliance never leads to the
deepest insights, only the will to simplicity does that.

One might say this much about Swoboda's laws of periodicity:
they are most readily demonstrated in the normal instance and
least in the pathological. The unconscious, here meaning the repressed, is, as it were, cramped by consciousness. On the one hand,
it is always present, although only in part, discordant and awry,
and, on the other hand, never rhythmically rising and falling in
fullness of expression. So one might imagine agreement between
Freud and Swoboda—or Freud and Fliess.[53]

I think it is fruitless to attempt to define specifically Weininger's[54] "masculine and feminine" principles. What the marriage
of opposites results in (child or work) *is* masculine–feminine; all
else are the very intermediate stages which lead to Swoboda's
"turbulently receptive cleavages."

I think that just because male and female are basic constituents
of *all* life, they both enter at some point into the formation of the
man as well as the woman. The often mentioned "war of the
sexes" in love comes about partly because we confuse the primary concepts of sexuality with actual living persons. In love-
making itself, i.e., when the sexes are most sharply differentiated,
where woman seems truly woman and man truly man, a recollection of one's own bisexual being seems to be awakened by the
opposite sex, as a consequence of the other's profound approach,
his understanding, and his embrace. In love and in submission

we are given the gift of ourselves, we are made more actual, more encompassing, more wedded to ourselves, and this alone is the true efficacy of love, giving life and joy. That is equally true for the second side of our being (male or female, respectively) which otherwise is likely to shrivel up and be suppressed, unchampioned in the struggle for existence. If we give ourselves, we possess ourselves entirely, in the image of the beloved—a seeming modesty!

I have found that every deep, worthwhile human relationship has this character and that it is a banal monstrosity to regard the sexes exclusively from one side. That is why "war" is the last word on the subject: the conquest of one by the other. Hence people are so horridly constricted into halves, into insensitive men who do not really experience the very dominion which they possess and into trampled women, who frequently to their own surprise bloom for the first time when they become widows —i.e., only then become the kind of person who might have been a refuge and an enchantment to a man. Only when there is a twofold alternation between masculinity and femininity can two persons be more than one, no longer regarding each other merely as a goal (like miserable halves which need to be stuck together to form a whole) but rather committed together to a goal outside themselves. Only then are love and creation, natural fulfillment and cultural activity no longer opposites, but one.

When people turn away from the erotic life, they develop the sign of the opposite sex notwithstanding, but now in distorted form: the man engaged in feminine activities and the emancipated woman.

I read somewhere in Fliess (whether or not it is really a fact, I do not know, since he often indulges in fantasy): "maturation" of ovum and sperm actually consists of a process whereby female substance from the sperm and male substance from the egg persist in the organizing body and thus enable the emergent individual to complete itself through the opposite sex.

Hence sexual attraction would in fact be a longing for our own self, displaced to the image of the partner. Anyhow, it is true for the psyche, and all we owe to our partner is our *thanks*.

DECEMBER 4, 1912

Wednesday Discussion: Freud on Adler

Practically a debate on Adler. Freud discoursed at length. His point of departure was his observation that penis envy may be present before "social" distinctions and comparisons are made and is therefore rooted in deeper levels than in the upper ones, which are the only levels Adler has considered (so that he imagines that everything is enacted on a single plane). The janitor's daughter envies the better-dressed banker's daughter upstairs, without becoming neurotic about it; more likely it is the latter who will later fall ill. Likewise there are throngs of wretches who have organic defects and no neurosis whatever.

Rosenstein spoke in behalf of Adler.

Hitschmann[55] too, to some extent: that the consciousness of inferiority is everywhere to be seen in the foreground of neurosis, so that patients feel that Adler's theory fits their case, and they feel relieved and understood (and pitied, said Tausk); but Adler's treatment comes to a halt before it reaches the neurosis itself, while Freud's exposes resistances instead (offering no quick relief). Adler was right being satisfied with the title of his book: *The Neurotic Constitution*.

Freud and Adler actually differ with regard to therapeutic method as the knife differs from salve. For the very reason that Adler works only on the basis of physiology and logic, *eo ipso* he does not try to effect any change in the physiologically based, logically unconscious states of mind. For example, an "arrangement" is manifest where compensation for a physical inferiority through ambition is "arranged" to ward off invidious comparison with others. But it is impossible to bring to consciousness the fact that such an exaggeration of self-esteem might have its roots in a disturbed sexual attitude toward others—simply because it is itself one of the arrangements of consciousness. This forcible self-isolation from real life which Adler, too, sees as so characteristic of all neurotics, has become a property of his own ideas. He turns realities into allegories (as a normal man does all the while to good effect, constructing his *raison d'être* on them) but in this process he treats the "arranger," the personality in question, as itself a fiction; it has no independent existence and can be involved with itself only through the "as if" of arrangements. The plane whence the personality arises to become ego, from whose unconscious layers the personality derives the broad reality underlying its conscious interpretations—this plane of Freud's real achievement is ignored and bypassed.

Consequently, Adler was unsuccessful some days later when in personal argument he made a vigorous attempt to convince me that the body's organ language and the ego's logical communications were one and the same so that between the two there was no room for the libido theory. I felt that his deficiency was one of *perceptiveness*. We had a passionate debate, finally going down all the streets at a run; he went along faithfully and touchingly.

DECEMBER 8, 1912

Visit to Freud: Natural Science—the Humanities

A visit to Freud on Sunday afternoon: very good for me, as we were able to come to grips with all the topics on which I had thought I disagreed and on which we are much closer than it had appeared. To see Freud thinking and at work is quite differ-

ent from merely reading him, although his books do represent
his personality clearly. We also talked about the seminar meeting
of the day before, and he conceded that many things had been
put crudely for the benefit of the crowd. As when in the case
of the matron he spoke of a quantitative increase in libido without mentioning other factors responsible for the failure of its
control, social rebuffs, injured self-esteem, and so forth; although
these latter might have won the day even if the libidinal quantum
had been less. (So Tausk's interruption on the stairs struck me as
correct when he preferred to think of a qualitative modification
of the libido.) I am not really convinced that such crudenesses
are harmless, quite apart from the fact that they lend some
seeming justice to Adler, illustrating the "deathly silence of the
ego instinct, the power instinct." They are dangerous above all
because scientific objections would here be justified: that the real
distinction between natural science and other scientific disciplines, e.g., between chemistry and psychology, becomes strikingly apparent here where the distinction is between things that
are quantifiable and those that are not, i.e., those which can only
be characterized qualitatively. This is such a great difference
that it inevitably must affect the method. In other words, we
must never forget that the use of the methods of quasiphysical
science in psychology is purely a matter of analogies. It is an unalterable fact that whatever lays claim to scientific validation
must be explained mechanistically and logically, and we have to
remain aware of the nonobjective nature of all the humanistic
disciplines. Still the best way to do that is within the context
of Freudian research. While in physiology, for example, and
psychophysics also—which is under its influence—we easily
overlook how unscientific ideas creep in along with the concept
of life itself, it is perfectly obvious that Freud's Ucs. cannot be
gotten at with levers and retorts. The fact that we can catch the
unconscious only in pathological material is proof of its undivided unity, intangible even in our most vital and individual

actions. This is just why Freud can forego all speculation and restrict himself exclusively to empirical data; on this account, too, the data are raised above the battle of contending opinion, even the changes in Freud's own opinions. What holds true for all the humanities is exceptionally valid here: we know only that which we experience.

South Slav Ballads

Tausk brought them to me in his translation. This is the poetry of which Goethe[56] said to Eckermann that it was the most beautiful he knew (or the like). It is really not enough to say that they are beautiful poems: they simply make you happy, and you react to them not so much with an opinion as with jubilation.

The delight that these people produce by brutality and cruelty —as befits their dimensions—is not due to a Nietzschean joy in the "blond beast" or mere primordial power, but rather depends on their profound awareness of the primordial power and its hierarchical order, limitations, and "sins"—but the sins are Promethean. (The naïve behavior of undomesticated animals is not to be found among these "savages," who are totally yoked to a religious ceremonial.)

Transgression and rebellion take place in the assumption of far more positive and more immediate consequences than our remote penalties in Hell or in the nearer but somehow more platonic bite of conscience. Since sin is something real to these people, it remains connected with the real events of life and hence finds its own vengeance. The sinner is thus at the same time a hero in that he surrenders to sin, he pays and he sacrifices, and he knows of the ecstasy which is the companion of the noblest deeds and sacrifices.

These people must therefore take quite a different position with regard to repression. Whatever brings revenge on itself directly *cannot first be repressed*, but remains in continuity with the usual course of nature; for good or ill one maintains one's own identity. Cowardice too only grows where there are corners to hide in, and it is generally acknowledged that animals of the open spaces develop more courage to act and courage to live than do those of the protecting forests.

So I keep returning to a problem which I find unjustly neglected by psychoanalysis. Namely, that when repressed and attenuated elements are released to consciousness, it must be a normal process for them to sink once more into the unconscious, to become fully effective only now through the release of their intrinsic energies. So plants that rot fully or dry out to dust once more come to life by supplying the earth with the manure without which it would become weary and unfruitful. We imagine the normal mind too exclusively as a vase of crystalline water filled with prettily arranged cut flowers, and we forget the black earth needed if roots are to grow. The man of the future is hence imagined to have practically an aseptic unconsciousness—and body and soul as sterile as could be. It is such a joy to become immersed in great folk poetry, which provides us with no sterilized material but only, and unworriedly, the very stuff of human life and being.

Folk poets are always right in making the kind of black and white qualitative distinctions which our poets with all their psychological training have so long transcended. More primitive poetry is by personal temperament devoted to telling of events and their effects; it has not yet compromised itself with science, which necessarily abstracts from them. The psychoanalytic attitude with its folklike mode of thinking is in accord with all this; it too returns to the typological forms and to the opposites inherent in them. It does this not out of any emotional or moral act of judgment, but on the contrary it is as pure as possible of such tendencies in deriving the individual elements from objective relations; while folk-thinking which does not elucidate conceptually stops with simplifications of that which it has subjectively perceived.

But there is still more to be said on the matter: the determinants revealed in psychoanalysis comprise only a single explanatory strand, not the entire structure but only the side which is directed toward us (as in the case of our life history, and so forth). To the extent that all this is a part of the totality of events and only exists because it is also actualized on the other side (turned away from our subjective awareness), we have roots in it, and it blossoms around us far beyond that which these few determinants permit us to see. The Ucs. has taught us that the true saying is that we *are*, rather than that *we* are, and ultimately it is not only emotional judgment, but beyond it objective judgment, that ceases at its deeper boundary. Here it is conceivable that the naïve primitive man accomplishes more than a comprehensive association when he puts himself involuntarily and without personal pretensions into the event within himself and around himself (human reactions and their conditions) as into a great selfsame unity. For an instant then he can act and think with greatness. It is something of the sort that moves us so deeply in these South Slav ballads, in the "deeds of sin," acts felt to be one's own true being, requiring no justification or special pleading, but simply affirming that which together with the act constitutes the eternal reality of events, although the consequence of the act may be destruction.

DECEMBER 9, 1912

Adler and Freud

Adler writes me complaining of Stekel's "disloyalty"—which I think is funny; it could not have been documented with greater speed. But he also complains of *mine*, and justly. We met and talked for two hours while racing all over town. But really it is perfectly possible to overcome all the differences between Freud and Adler insofar as Adler's feeling of inferiority already comprises a primal repression experienced as a basic slight, and also insofar as Freud's "repressed" is founded on psychized material which had already in the past attained consciousness. If we call this material "sexual" we do so by assuming it to be distinguished from "mental"; the two belong together to emphasize their duality. On the other hand, when Adler emphasizes the "ego protest," he does so only by contrasting it with the murky totality which in a certain sense is sexuality. The mark of sexuality is that it may be viewed from two sides, from both the mental and the physical; it is here where all mental disorders and neuroses meet, as if at the point of intersection which exemplifies the whole. But only Freud has appropriated the word "compromise" for this, and only he has done justice to the double character of the process, even though he has predominantly emphasized the sexual side (especially in the beginning, when hysteria was under consideration). Only he has uncovered the intermediate range of unconscious mental functions, and only thereby has he succeeded in making room for the positive mechanisms of the process; and only this is important. Beyond merely elucidating illness, and led that far by the pathological process, we find our way into the mystery of the normal unconscious state, in which sexuality and the ego maintain their narcissistic union and the true enigma of mankind begins. For Adler there can be no enigma strictly speaking; he sees the ego confronted only by its own game.

DECEMBER 11, 1912

Wednesday Discussion: the Personal Element in Philosophy

Winterstein's[57] paper was excessively praised, even applauded with bravos—just because he did not meddle with anyone else's business as most papers ordinarily do, ending in a confused battle over priority with everyone staking out the same claim.

There were some very good passages in it; for example, to what degree the libido originally extended to everything and later became concentrated on individuals (actually the concept of love), so that a variety of things that were realities in the past now appear as mere symbols.

Freud said by way of conclusion that we might explain consciousness, as compared with sensory apprehension of the external world, as the function which makes qualitative distinctions based on the quantities established by perception.

I liked his other characteristic remark that if he had to confess to any philosophic position, he would hold with the least misgiving to a kind of dualism.

Whoever, like Freud, eschews philosophy, reveals a truly philosophic mind by repudiating the whole monistic babble and laying hold of the breadth and depth of empirical reality, which is demonstrably dualistic.

Winterstein's view was in essence that it is the task of psychoanalysis to show how philosophical systems arise from the nature of their founders, as that nature is disclosed by psychoanalysis. So much can be conceded. Still, it might be added that to subject the emanations of one's own personality to objective validation means something quite different today from what it meant a decade ago when it would have been confronted by the arrogant pretensions of metaphysics.

The personal element is now recognized as normative in even the most abstract thought, and if it is not depersonalized it plays a considerably more robust and muscular role in the synthesis of objective truth. The recognition of things not only in their subjective appearance but also as they are tasted, experienced, and performed—in a word, brought to life—has become a matter of style and technique. We come to suspect that this kind of evaluation, seemingly so personal, is not so remote from the truth as we assumed it to be during the time when logic was so overesteemed. Just as the affective element, selectively commanding our attention, is essential to ideation and to logical thought, so, conversely, ultimate values—the personally comprehensible values of life— are beginning to disclose the knowledge of being.

It is only in the age of psychoanalysis that this insight would have to prevail. Never before have we felt as we do now that our knowledge depends so much on what we are and that our being has been released from its narrowly personal confines into the depth and the breadth behind us, which is one with life itself, indistinguishable from ourselves. The old philosophic adage "know thyself" is no longer just an ethical matter but one of life itself, and it involves less the knowledge of our obligations than of our existence.

Daily in the neurological outpatient clinic with Tausk, through the courtesy of Frankl-Hochwart, the director of the clinic, who has permitted us to analyze from nine in the morning until one o'clock in the afternoon—in white doctors' smocks. A frightful case of a paranoid woman; although Tausk wore himself out trying to get a postponement, she has already been committed to the asylum.

Lecture: Therapy of the Neuroses—Transference—Intellect and Affect

The last meeting before Christmas vacation. Freud must be glad; he even made a slip and said "before the end of the semester."

On the therapy of the neuroses: it is successful when the libidinal gain of the neurosis has become superfluous. We are forced to the following conclusion: the libidinal gain of a neurosis derives from the fact that it is expressed psychically. We feel that *physical* illnesses proceed at our expense and that they might be profitable to the tumor or the calcification but not to ourselves. On the other hand, even the maddest and most distorted creation or transformation of the psyche, although of no use whatsoever, still remains an assertion of our self, on which account any attempt at a cure is bound at first to mean defeat and depression. Even the sickest mental life is still "life" with all its marvels, so that one cannot encroach on it forcibly without appearing to injure it and diminish it.

On the *transference*. It should not work merely in the presence of suggestion, which in neurotics is limited by the ambivalent attitude. Hence we need to weaken the resistance by the psychoanalytic method of bringing things to consciousness and communicating them with the aid of the transference. On the other hand, it is futile just to make the unconscious conscious, since it only has affective significance through the agency of the transference, of confident trust. Here by the word "transference" Freud only means "respect" or affection, even when he means transference to a paternal object; he makes no mention of its sexual root, which was so shocking to Bjerre[58] that he rejected the whole theory of the transference. It seems to me that the sexual root of the transference, where all sympathy lies, attains a most peculiar flowering in the case of the neurotic, since he has regressed so deeply into the infantile where the psychic roots impinge on their physical ground.

According to Freud's view of *the dependence of intellectual function on emotions* we might conclude that what we call the creativity of genius is liberated as resistances break down. The commonplace individual would have no such resistances to overcome; the neurotic would be unable to overcome them. In the creative person it is the steady increase of his spiritual functioning to new levels, by means of the loosening of its structure, that culminates in creativity. Just as illness needs to reach out for cure, so the healthy mind should confidently submit to the risk of loosening and transformation. For our inner vitality is no less endangered by the walls that confine it than by the abyss beneath; petrifaction is death just as surely as disintegration. But instead of the pain and misery which might urge the neurotic to find healing, it is avoidance of pain and the quest for a paltry ease that restrain the healthy mind. Yet life is only truly life when it signifies not comfort but procreation, a synthesis of pain and happiness, misery and bliss.

Analyst and Analysand

Tausk says (and besides him only Gebsattel[59]) that analytic treatment alienates the persons involved in it, while most people stress the risk of sexual countertransference. He says also that our piecemeal method of investigation does not lead to an overall picture of the individual. There are of course two basic reasons for this: for one thing, surgical incisions of a face do not improve its beauty, and furthermore, individualized modes of expression yield to a generalized type when the underlying strata are exposed. We have a single common unconscious just as we have a single anatomical structure. (This awakens our sympathy too, but in another way.) But I think there is a third factor inherent in the use of the method itself. There is an unalterable contradiction in the application of a method derived from science—the logical analysis by which we gain control of the outer world—to the immediate data of our inmost experiences. It is not simply a question of inspecting psychic life from the outside, a matter of "psychology" so to speak, but rather an invasion and a definition of its spontaneous flow *in vivo;* the analyst participates actively, not just by understanding. It is therefore a purely artificial expression to speak of "determination" when it is the meaning of life in its totality that is at stake. That can be experienced only as a *unity*, and yet here it must be submitted to an incongruous method of disentanglement into a chain of component links. Each link is deprived of the claim that it is, in its vital impetus, what Nietzsche called "the whole lineage of mankind up unto itself."

Along with all the resistances which derive from the mental content that is to be analyzed from the unresolvable pathological fragments, there is bound to be another specific resistance from the total form of man's inner life. Possibly this would be strongest in the healthy person and would demand the strongest sort of transference as a counterforce, since in such a moment only the total integrity of another person could offer assurance of solace and rescue.

The great advantages of listening to the life of the mind in its own terms, unmodified by physiological ones inherently foreign to it, are naturally limited by the fact that we have to submit our findings to the point of view of logic, acquired through our observation of the external world. And that is why the individual who undertakes analysis with us does not behave more sympathetically, but seems rather to disguise himself anew. If the method permitted otherwise, as unhappily it does not, we would approach the analysand in his totality as we approach the components: then we would not meet with just a few monotonously

repetitious basic elements when the analysis ends in the unconscious depth, but we would sink beyond it into the mutely
solemn miracle of a world that is our own world, inexhaustible
just because it is our common life. The final result would not be
in elements of pathologic guilt, which ideally yield to cure, but
in an all-comprising guiltlessness. The all-too-human structure
revealed in its indigent nakedness would be wrapped in a shining
white mantle, the mantle of narcissism. After so many disguises
have been torn from our personal destiny, and so many idealized
facts destroyed, we should be able to go on long enough together
to reach the point where the individual can humble himself
quietly and see through his own absurd ambitions. For at that
time he is raised and restored to his homeland, to his total value, in
which he can remain undisturbed and can utter only one judgment on the value of human effort: "They know not what they
do."

Recently Tausk commented on the nearly exclusive involvement of Jews in the progress of psychoanalysis. It was understandable, he said, that we could see the fabric more clearly in
ancient and dilapidated palaces through their crumbling walls
and could gain insights which remain hidden in fine new houses
with smooth façades revealing only their color and their outward shape.

Spinoza

It is surely not rare for a person to discover in his early
years the expressed form of what is most deeply personal to himself. This happened to Tausk too in the case of Spinoza, on whom
he had written an essay in 1907. Also, significantly, he had never
known Spinoza fully hitherto nor read him *in toto*. It is a quality
of Spinoza that a few pages by him can teach us whether we are
his disciples, whereas big interpretive works have been written

about him based on the most erudite misunderstandings. For to think like him does not mean to adopt a system but just to think.

The word "representation" which first came up at a Wednesday meeting as Tausk's own, is quite characteristic of his inner allegiance to Spinoza. To grasp Spinoza it is only necessary to think through to its conclusion the concept that physical and mental manifestations are representations of one another. That is quite a different thing from systematic parallelism, which the deepest wisdom now styles as "cerebral localization" and the like. It is rather the conscious inward contemplation of the integrity and presentness of two worlds—as we reckon—which nowhere exclude or determine each other, because they *are but one*. It is the philosophical step that goes beyond Freud; he has developed throughout a method of its own for the one of these two worlds which can be grasped psychologically. It had always been applied to the other one.

A fundamental principle of psychoanalysis supports Spinozism very powerfully—the concept of *overdetermination*. This insight, that everything is, nay *must*, be psychically overdetermined if only one pursues it far enough, reaches far beyond the usual logical concept of determination, splits its one-sided concatenation, and ultimately turns it into a principle of universal reciprocity. The reciprocal interaction of everything with everything else needs only to be assumed with all its implications to come, along with Spinoza, from the empirical world of movement to the eternal rest of his philosophy. This exalted repose means at the same time the most passionate ecstasy, never possessed by any thinker to such a degree as by this one perhaps who, stammeringly, gave the same meaning to "nature" and "God," yet without supernaturalizing nature or reducing the name of his God to the level of things.

It delights me that the one thinker I approached in my childhood and almost adored now meets me once again, and as the philosopher of psychoanalysis. Think far enough, correctly enough on any point at all and you hit upon him; you meet him waiting for you, standing ready at the side of the road.

Christmas

Spent Christmas with Ellen at Beer-Hofmann's;[60] for a few days before also with him and again right after Christmas. Beer-Hofmann has become more than a mere memory, and I am touched how it has become just that for him. In the past a gay and easy-going wanderer through the world, now he is sedentary and melancholy and could not be further from the things that used to delight me and cheer me in those serious days of mine. Still in his retrospective sharing of my pleasure there was something strangely moving from the very start of the visit. It sounds absurd to say that he looks at me as a grownup looks at a childish person; but as I sat there on Christmas eve in front of the tiny ornamented tree that burned on my plate as if it were Tom Thumb's very own, it really seemed as if the man wanted to bestow a present with every glance and was awaiting the return of a neglected joy.

Alcohol and Homosexuality

Conversations with Tausk, on the typical alcoholic, who is homosexually disposed, does not masturbate, is primitive and explosive in relation to women, acutely excitable—quite analogous in all this to the self-loving, self-asserting person who is inconstant to objects and has little sexual desire. But in this case intoxication summons forth what happens normally in the other. Furthermore, alcohol raises self-esteem and, by removing inhibitions, counteracts many depressions. (Hence perhaps it is that after the atrophy or removal of the thyroid it is possible to tolerate so much alcohol with ease and that in cases of hypertrophy of this organ of stimulation through secretion there is intolerance to alcohol.) They only turn to alcohol to attain by artificial means the state in which the healthy and contented man exists normally. Whence the question whether homosexuality in alcoholics is not often something different from true homosexuality, not so much a disinclination toward woman as a search for pleasure in oneself and a consequent self-affirmation through the person of the same sex. As a matter of fact, the alcoholic does approach women. Frequently his homosexuality is only apparent; that is, it is founded less on sexual peculiarities than within the domain of the ego. That is also worth thinking about with regard to compulsion neurosis and the propensity to doubting, on which Freud says: "What is characteristic of this neurosis—what differentiates it from hysteria—is not, in my opinion, to be found in instinctual life, but in the psychological field." [61]

Psychological relations of this kind could easily lead to a masochistic organization and result—in the attempt to correct such a character lacking the instinctual disposition to it—in a man's turning toward man, while his sexual attitude toward woman, in the physiological sense, remained intact.

JANUARY 11, 1913

Lecture: Dream and Fairy Tale

Right after the holidays we began with real fairy tales and in the presence of many guests. He did a superb job, using the dreams of the seven wolves and of Rumpelstiltskin torn in two. I was sorry not to have brought Ellen with me. Afterward Freud sent Ferenczi and me to the Ronacher Café where we waited in vain for the others and then started on a very thorough discussion of some ideas Ferenczi is working on. On the way home, looking

through the big plate glass windows, I could see the others sitting
in the Alserhof; I went in and witnessed the debate between
Tausk and Dr. Seif[62] of Munich. Rank, Hitschmann, and the
others kept neutral. Tausk certainly speaks at his best in replying
to someone; here, too, even in abstract thought, he comes back to
the living person. It would be impossible to change a single
word of his or to be clearer or more judicious. But it is beginning
to be plain that any purely factual deliberation about Jung gets
very complicated on account of the need to overlook differences in the interest of unity. A dangerous question. Tausk's
first-rate reply made Rank suspicious of him.

The telegrams awaiting me at home.[63]

Night, still and solemn.

JANUARY 15, 1913

Wednesday Discussion: Magic and Religion

Freud's paper on magic.[64] Ferenczi still present and Tausk
needlessly picking a quarrel with him during the discussion. Together until two in the morning at the Ronacher Café. Freud
promised to give me the galley proofs of the paper. During the
afternoon, when Ferenczi was at my place, we took up a work of
his which he showed me in manuscript. It touches on the nature
of religion much as I myself see it, but only from an external
view; to me the essence of religious thought is that in it man
merges himself with the powers of the outer world. He needed
to do that as soon as consciousness forced him to recognize his
distance from the outside world, so much more than the animals,
which remain in instinctive union with it. In *magical* invocation
man naïvely feels godlike, by deriving his own origin from the
divine; in religion, on the other hand, by objectifying the gods,
he makes them to be like men. The two together represent the

eruption of a confidence at once childlike and creative. It is the fictions that evolve from them that serve as a crutch and foundation for feelings of insecurity and inferiority.

Only half here, living with my dead Muschka. No one knows about her, so that no one can touch this (here where no one knew her, and yet everyone would have to say something.)

Lecture: Two Lies Told by Children[65]

A little girl brags, shows off, and lies out of love for her father, a skilled draftsman, by pretending in school that she has drawn freehand a circle that actually was made with a compass. He is an impecunious merchant, and on the way to school she boasted about having ice cream at dinner. (She said they always had ice cream at home—but she really knew nothing about ice cream.) In her neurosis in later life the "ice" appeared in a phobia for shattered glass. A *stranger* gave her a doll as a present; she not only took it without grace or gratitude but she let it fall out of the doll carriage at the first opportunity so that it broke its head. Her father gave her her only spanking on account of this, yet this was totally forgotten, even during analysis and was subsequently recalled only with the mother's aid. Her father suspected neither her identification with him nor "the rescue fantasy" that motivated her immoral behavior (her lying, to make him important and to rescue him). Progress in analysis came about through the father-transference. First came depreciation; she remained "ill" in order to love him thereafter, to rescue him by bragging about her cure by Freud.

Freud told me that her neurosis broke out when she realized that she had no hope of a child by her husband ("the father").

Easter egg coloring day. Theft of the fifty heller, which her father had refused her and which came to her as change out of a school contribution toward a funeral wreath. Her brother, thinking of himself as "better" than she, betrayed her. The punishment, because it was administered by her mother and not by her father, brought about a total alteration in her character, just as in the first case. She did it all in order to be physically chastised by her father, interpreting the spanking as the kind of sexual caresses he gave her mother during coitus. Having as a little child observed her nurse's sexual intercourse with a doctor, she was accustomed to accept pennies for candy as "hush money." Later on money was something bad she threw into the street. (As a patient she had the association "Judas Iscariot's pieces of silver.") Gradually developed the neurotic association of money and sexual pleasure—oversensitivity, conflicts.

JANUARY 21, 1913

Woman's Cultural Attainments

Tuesday in Tausk's course I was struck by a remark and we argued about it all the way home with Dr. Jekels. He said quite characteristically that "even" men prefer to remember the path to sexual pleasure rather than the goal and turn their attention away from the act itself as from something embarrassing. Perhaps it is not "even" but especially true of men and with good reason, since for them cultural upbringing is nearly identical with a bad conscience attendant on wish-fulfillment. Of course this is not the case for a great many men and an even greater number of women. And that too has good reasons. For it is really woman's only cultural attainment that she isolates sexuality from her experience less than man is able to do. Hence she no longer needs to find it coarse and demanding to be repressed, simply because in the sexual act woman surrenders her personality, as it were. In this respect—not in every respect—she shows a masochistic organization and hence must not be ashamed of the act if she is to survive it at all. She devotes all the strength of her civilization (which man employs elsewhere) to the end of cultivating this one attainment for the assimilation of the whole drive. One might even suspect that a woman who needs to make too much of the claims of fidelity, ethics, marriage, and the like, so as *not* to be ashamed, is already in conflict in having to justify her own instinctual life. That is, she has come to think too poorly of herself and requires a sanction. It might really be an excuse for a less faithful woman to say that she did not conserve sufficient energy to have any left for morality, simply because she has so lavishly poured out into the festival of love all of the best she knew. She saves nothing out of the erotism of the hour, that might serve to build houses, but into it she has put everything that ever was called loneliness. No bonds are forged this way which might compete with the chains of marriage, but there is no limit to the available forms into which her erotism might flow without limit—as sister, mother, comrade, child—and continue to be strong and unpretentious by the very fact that she accepts unquestioningly the fact of its existence.

JANUARY 22, 1913

Wednesday Discussion: the Miner of Salun

Little Dr. Lorenz[66] gave a paper, very erudite but also a trifle tiresome. Freud's concluding remarks made up for it. He found a couple of motifs in fairy tales analogous to the miner's tale in the lecture, and they suddenly acquired a burning psychological interest. The study of the "widowed bride"—of the miner —presented as an incident so embarrassing that the motivations were transformed into a conflict between vocation and love which seemed closely intertwined. Also "mother earth" (here receiving the dead unharmed) is seen in its original brutal and real meaning by which burial might be understood to mean rejuvenation. Consequently, the frequently deplored burial alive of old people may not be a horror after all! Reitler's[67] good observation on the carbuncle stone, which is often invisible, and Freud's additional comment that this property is negatively demonstrated by conferring on others the capacity of becoming invisible. Lively discussion.

I thought once more as I have so often thought, that quite apart from the worth of the individual papers we are in such good company here. With Freud presiding and with the unobtrusive guidance he gives to it all, a better quality of work results than a corresponding number of more important minds might produce. One would like to invite the best of minds to attend these evenings, and one is grateful to sit beside Freud.

JANUARY 25, 1913

Lecture: the Neurotic, the Healthy Man

Neurotic types met with in treatment. It appeared that the world is indeed less in need of improvement and less capable of it than one might think. One finds types whose socially harmful instincts have developed in such intimate union with their most valuable ones, that one might at best strive only for a better distribution of the forces than that which took place in their childhood. Or conversely those types in which one sees not so much the neurotic patient as a neurotic world; they would only need courage to attain their natural development within their unnatural milieu, but with it they would destroy this milieu too. So, in the end most things are best as they are. It all had a weary tone but Freud can speak differently too.

The seriously disturbed patient is the one who can be most profoundly influenced, his need being the greatest; the mildly afflicted less so; and least of all the healthy person who could if he but chose increase his insight and his strength by means of analysis.

But who is this healthy man, by the foregoing account so melancholy and resigned? Freud said Wednesday that the backwardness of "savages" seems to go hand in hand with their uninhibited sexual enjoyment, just as after puberty a diminution of intellectual acuteness sets in after early and abundant gratification. In that case the neurotic compromise blocking enjoyment with a dark feeling of guilt would have some justification in its own subtle and yet misleading way. It would be justified in its attempt to do right by *both* sides—nature *and* culture; but such a consideration would demand that we understand by "health" not the cultural antithesis, but the unity of the two—cultural life itself being a level of personal development. Every "savage" has accomplished that too in his own way. It is this accomplishment that determines the value of health, when rigidity of convention, on the one hand, or ineffectual modification of the instincts, on the other, has not led to defeat. Furthermore, it causes the production of neurotic guilt feelings to appear as a kind of "moral obligation to be healthy"—no doubt itself pathogenic, but coming from a longing for health that is superior to a commonplace comfort.

Sexuality and Ego

While Tausk's concept of neurosis—as expressed in conversation at the *Alte Elster*—is the same as Freud's, he emphasized the "failure" in the sphere of the ego, and hence in the social sphere, as an absolutely necessary condition for the outbreak of neurosis. Whence refuge will be taken in sexuality and illness becomes manifest when disharmony ensues. At least that is what I understood him to mean. The fundamental cause continues to be sexual, and it was to be expected that a disharmony between sexual instincts and ego instincts is a probable antecedent for the later brutal appearance of such a disturbance of the equilibrium. One must think one's way right down to the root in the narcissistic phase where both instincts are undivided and still at rest in each other.

In Freud's earlier writings narcissism is certainly not so clearly distinguished from autoerotism as is now the case. It was only through Tausk's formulations that I personally became clear about the equal significance of ego and sex, and yet Freud is now in accord. To my mind this equality alone makes conceivable the possibility of the process of sublimation; if the ego instinct originally had an equal share, then a rearrangement of sexuality to the ends determined by the ego is not excluded. Before this was clear Adler had, through misunderstanding, some justification for his notion, namely that the ego employs sexuality merely symbolically for its own guiding purpose. But now light is cast on the heart of the matter (which Adler reduces to a disembodied psychic game), namely the true mutuality of the psyche with the source of its conscious organization.

Personal observation has convinced me that everything created by dreams and delusions, simply because the gaze is directed inwardly rather than outwardly, appears as if viewed through a magnifying glass—one which sometimes produces monstrous distortions and sometimes turns into the grandiose. It is as if all the individualizing and limiting elements, toward which reason and perception are directed, give place more and more to the onslaught of the unbounded totality of a world that is mirrored in all of us in the narcissistic state of dreaming.

Still Freud is right in looking to sexuality for the unifying factor of the mental processes, since it is there that we come on the ultimate abode of the personal. If we experience suffering the decision seems to be made there whether we shall be able to master it. Although we are turned from the sphere of the ego by a sort of dissolution of the self, we are still able to find out down there that our roots are undisturbed and that we can grow tall again and bloom and bear fruit in our ego. It is also significant that pleasure and pain alternate freely within sexuality as they do whenever procreative processes run their course; asexual non-erotic individuals who are generally much less sensitive to pain, conversely must also get along without the most mysterious of consolations. In the narcissistic stage, man learns for certain that pain and pleasure can actually become identical like all pairs of opposites. This is also our discovery at those moments when pain in all its fury becomes an outburst of life that takes us along with it and not a suffering that diminishes us, or when joy goes to such extreme that it cannot any longer be pleasurable. In Goethe's words:

> The undying gods give all,
> All, to their beloved,
> An infinity of pleasure,
> An infinity of pain.[68]

Postscript: The drive for self-assertion can only negate pain. When it is no longer effective to do so, sexuality (the drive to surrender) can still turn pain into sensual pleasure and include even death as a desideratum. Hence any excessive degree of sensation, even the most frightfully unpleasurable one, stimulates sexuality. And for the same reason the happiness which accompanies the drive for self-assertion is effective for only a little while before it comes to resemble pain.

JANUARY 28, 1913

Tausk's Course: the Concept of Censorship

Lectures on the dream concluded and those on sexuality begun. Very clearly demonstrated with reference to the dream of the two rats, how dreams must offer sexual problems and can stammer their meaning to us only in a sexual language since they attain consciousness only via the body so to speak, and are articulated in its words.

On the way home argued with Tausk and Dr. Jekels on the concept of censorship. Freud does not stick closely now to his original definition, as I was so impressed in one of the lecture sessions at the beginning of the winter. I have always thought that the essential censorship was already accomplished by the symbolic nature of the latent dreamwork generally, which *eo ipso* must lead to gross distortions in relation to consciousness. But in addition it seems to me that whenever *inhibitions* might collaborate in a distorting expression, they might very well originate in the unconscious on the basis of forgetting which followed obscurely and not just from the *compromise* with waking thoughts directed by consciousness.

It would be a very good thing to make a clear distinction between Freud's concept of censorship and Adler's "guide lines" and safeguards. In the form of primary safeguards they are of course uncensored, being simply overcompensations. But as secondary ones, aimed as protective devices against the bold exaggerations of the primary safeguards, they imply a concept of censorship. Characteristically they descend from above only in appearance, for it is easily seen that the hidden instinctual life once again makes its way into the second class of safeguards. All of which is accounted for as inferiority before it needs to be compensated. In other words it is clear that the secondary safeguards imply Freud's repressed in disguise (disguised for example as "the feminine means," whereas it is actually the feminine goal in itself). Naturally I could not convince Adler when we debated about it. We fight like mad.

Wednesday Discussion: Periodicity—Object- and Subject-Erotism—Symbol Formation

Evening of reports. Rosenstein on Fliess's periodicity. Freud replied at great length about his scientific relations with Fliess and how after Fliess had brought the matter of bisexuality to his attention he later on had to hold on to this as his own discovery. On the occasion of his break with Fliess: the difference in their methods, psychological instead of organismic.

Federn remarked—and I think it is certainly so—that periodicity is more clearly evident in normal or convalescent cases, while in the pathological instance it is more concealed or else displaced. It is in fact only one expression of the rhythmic automatism that proceeds where everything "works." That is how the inner life looks to us, when we imagine it to be automatic, i.e., mechanistically explicable, organically (or in the last analysis: cosmically) represented. How incomparably alive it is then in its real, *immediate*, mental manifestations! Conversely, when the inner life is disturbed in its outer progress, it is much harder to grasp; and for that reason it becomes more automatic in its mental manifestations and therefore approachable by psychoanalysis and treatable.

Freud, on Tausk's clinical discussion of dreams: a dream symbol can be at once male and female because it is infantile and so came to exist before the differentiation of the sexes, or the dreamer is homosexually disposed and the symbol is hence transposed.

Tausk, on Sadger's views: that he had not adequately distinguished between subject- and object-erotism so that there was a logical confusion. One might accordingly speak of mouth- or mucous-membrane-erotism when implying the erotic subject, but not of buttocks-erotism since the term refers to the libidinal object. At the close of the discussion Freud referred favorably to this clarifying observation—having immediately forgotten who had made it. He then smilingly apologized for his error.

Meanwhile he undertook a polemic against Adler in a manner which struck me as open to misunderstanding. He emphasized that the formation of symbols takes place at two levels: out of the unconscious and out of the rationalization of the unconscious— Adler always having only the second in mind. But this surely is not the whole thing. Adler likewise wants to discriminate his "guiding tendencies" from the rationalizations of them; he simply looks at them from the side of their psychic structure instead of that of their instinctual content. Consequently he always talks about what the *psyche* does with *them*, whereas Freud keeps in mind what *they* do with the *psyche*. They are both speaking of the same thing inasmuch as sexuality is at first the only external manifestation of the bodily element, and correspondingly sexuality can be manifested as such only through the agency of the psychic tendency asserted by it.

I think that the physical has first rank in the formation of symbols if only because it provides the earliest images and continues to be more capable of pictorial representation.

FEBRUARY 2, 1913

A Visit to Freud: the Narcissistic Cat—Psychoanalysis as a Gift

Spent Sunday afternoon until evening at Freud's. This time much more personal conversation, during which he told me of his life, and I promised to bring photographs next time. Most personal of all perhaps was his charming account of the "narcissistic cat." While Freud maintained his office on the ground floor, the cat had climbed in through the open window. He did not care much for cats or dogs or animals generally, and in the beginning the cat aroused mixed feelings in him, especially when it climbed down from the sofa on which it had made itself comfortable and began to inspect in passing the antique objects which he had placed for the time being on the floor. He was afraid that by chasing it away he might cause it to move recklessly in the midst of these precious treasures of his. But when the cat proceeded to make known its archaeological satisfaction by purring and with its lithe grace did not cause the slightest damage, Freud's heart melted and he ordered milk for it. From then on the cat claimed its rights daily to take a place on the sofa, inspect the antiques, and get its bowl of milk. However, despite Freud's increasing affection and admiration, the cat paid him not a bit of attention and coldly turned its green eyes with their slanting pupils toward him as toward any other object. When for an instant he wanted more of the cat than its egoistic-narcissistic purring, he had to put his foot down from his comfortable chaise and court its attention with the ingenious enticement of his shoe-toe. Finally, after this unequal relationship had lasted a long time without change, one day he found the cat feverish and gasping on the sofa. And although it was most painstakingly treated with hot fomentations and other remedies, it succumbed to pneumonia, leaving naught of itself behind but a symbolic picture of all the peaceful and playful charm of true egoism.

Freud also talked about why I had become so deeply involved in psychoanalysis. To begin with, it was nothing but the kind of neutral objective interest that one feels when embarking on new researches. Then the opportunity came in all its liveliness and personal urgency to stand in the presence of a new science, again and again to be at a beginning and thus related to the problems of the science in an increasingly intimate way. What settled the matter for me, however, was the third and most personal reason that psychoanalysis bestowed a gift on me personally, its radiant enrichment of my own life that came from slowly groping the way to the roots by which it is embedded in the totality. When Freud said laughingly "I really think you look on analysis as a sort of Christmas present," I could only agree, since for me it was not a question of resolving conflicts between the depth and the surface. And quite possibly neither joy nor anguish are ever so vividly impressed on us as when they proceed from the unconscious to the level of experience; just as bliss once enjoyed can be horribly transformed into pain in the course of the night, so too it is likely that the memory of hours of crucifixion may be transformed to a life beyond, a resurrection glistening with the stars. In the homeland of our emotional life it is true that heaven and hell—in other respects only fictions—are preserved for us in the unconscious as our eternal reality.

FEBRUARY 5, 1913

Wednesday Discussion: Childhood Sexuality—Muscular Erotism

Freud talked about how he had come to the assumption of childhood sexuality. Originally proceeding from analytic practice, where there were presented many analogies with the sexual feelings of adults. Subsequently it turned out that neurotics in particular confirmed this fact by reproducing their early memories in strongly sexualized forms. But after this observation seemed to make the whole question of childhood sexuality a debatable one, the *normal* experiences of childhood were shown to be tied so intimately to the later events of normal sexuality that they had to be recognized as essentially related. (It is obviously all the same whether we take sexuality in adults as a rather more comprehensive concept than is customary or infantile sexuality in a rather narrower sense.) A more precise statement of the concept might gradually be established with the corroboration of other pertinent sciences. One ought not to cling dogmatically to definitions in view of the interconnections of the individual sciences and their contributions. (Hearing Freud speak thus one appreciates not only the self-imposed restraint implicit in such words but also the investigator's delicate pleasure in sticking calmly to positive fact.) Returning to the subject of "muscular erotism" (on which Sadger lectured the previous Wednesday), Freud observed further: Sadger's kind of logical inaccuracy, throwing subject and object together, is interestingly vindicated in pathological states. In hysteria there really is something like muscle- and buttocks-erotism, since the object becomes subject by means of conversion—a stiff leg becoming the penis, and so on. But in general—and here he dismissed Sadger in principle—the muscles, like all other organs, are executive organs and are not to be confused with the affect itself, that is with its psychological side through which the gentlest muscular contraction, or even a mere glance, can release more violent excitement than the wildest brawl or the hardest physical work. So also in sports and the like, one must always take into account that they can function sexually (in Sadger's sense) or entirely asexually, depending on whether bodily activity is or is not permitted to serve as the executive of the libido.

FEBRUARY 8, 1913

Lecture: Traumas of Childhood

Went with Beer-Hofmann, who had just visited me. On traumas of childhood. Not important in themselves. An unsheltered child exposed to all manner of traumas might often remain healthier if his later way of life is untroubled than a protected

one, who in later life is confronted by greater cultural renuncia-
tions and who in order to find some kind of sexual outlet must
regress to the few meager childhood memories that had been his
lot too and *retrospectively raise these to the level of actual traumas.* These are the cases, where a mere delay at the chamber pot or
the disrobing of some person or other becomes significant as the
releasing mechanism for much later neuroses. So far the "princely
education along psychoanalytic lines" has not accomplished much,
since the child brings its sexuality along with it all the same and
has to dispose of it somehow. Childhood traumas only play their
true role as substitutive complexes. The self-control and self-
denial imposed on the child are not merely those of moral culture.
Hygiene and cleanliness even earlier require considerable repression of the sexual on behalf of the aesthetic. (One has to recall
that the coprophilic inclinations of neurotics are those of their
primary sexuality.)

Still, his conclusion slipped back into the unreconciled opposition between nature and culture, whereby the individual's lib-
eration only results in conflict, since freedom has meaning only
as freedom of everybody.

The majority, however, agreed with him more and left with
greater enthusiasm than after the two child analyses two weeks
ago, when unconcealed expressions of indignation were to be
heard as the whole band struggled homeward through the wintry
gardens. When I do not accompany Freud, Tausk and I like to
listen in on the conversation of the others on their way home.
This time on the way there with Beer-Hofmann.

Childhood, Ego, and World

Whenever the discussion turns, as it often does, to the significance for the child of the first intimations of the sexual behavior of the parents, I recall an event out of my very early years.

I was sleeping beside the wall of the bedroom, my parents' beds standing out from the rear wall into the room. Awakening one night I discovered by the feeble light that shone from the street that my father's bed, the one next to mine, was empty. My impression was: he is gone, i.e., no longer there, *dead*—a death in no wise connected with a corpse, which would still be *there*. It made me so unhappy that I began to cry in my fright. Then I heard a moan from the other bed a little further distant from me and not lighted by the feeble lights. From that I concluded that my mother if not already dead must be dying, and I let out a horrible shriek. When both my parents came rushing in a panic to my bed, all I could tell them amid terrifying howls was that I had become an orphan. Their physical presence was quite ineffective to set me right.

With regard to my brothers, concerning whom Freud questioned me during our evening *à deux* on the second of February, it so happened they were much older than I, even the youngest being older by three years, and their conduct toward me was very chivalrous and protective. Aside from a few scuffles with the youngest, our daily dealings with one another were such that later when I left Russia as a young girl I looked on all the world as if it were populated by brothers alone. This was responsible for the openness and trustfulness I have had toward all men all my life, and it has never been deceived. Yet it is most striking that in spite of having such brothers, whose sister I am still today proud and happy to be, and in spite of the harmonious marriage of my parents and their pious constancy extending to their children as well, I was nevertheless miserably lonely with all of them and closely devoted to my fantasy life as my only joy; so too my later way of life and my wonderful later youth was in strongest contrast to everything at home.

Sunday afternoon, February 9, I talked about these things further with Freud. My childhood idea of woman's internal organs: like the inside of the mountains filled with precious stones (an early trip to Switzerland, aged two and a half, with a look at the Jungfrau; descent into a mine near Salzburg with my father). My first favorite fairy tale was the one about the princess from whose mouth jewels gushed with every word (frogs to begin with, I think). To this day the Russian word for pearl, жемчуг, has a peculiarly tender and delicate sound for me. But my very first memory of jewels was of my mother's box full of many-colored fancy glass buttons.

It was wonderful to arrive in the Syringgasse in the evening with flowers from Freud, to be greeted at the door by Tausk's two boys and presented with a vase full of water for the roses.

Freud also talked about Stekel and his methodological leaps. I long thought that his concept "polymorphous criminality" was a colossal exaggeration until I realized that there is inevitably an emotion analogous to hate at the onset of all conscious awareness. We attain our separate individuality only by repelling something and being repelled by it. If hate and the doom of death are found in the underworld of dreams, that only betokens the first point of departure—the first chilling isolation and separation without which an ego would no more come to be than would pulmonary respiration without the interruption of the direct supply of oxygen from the maternal body. Primary hate is not originally directed against something *other;* it is anxiety about one's self, the anxiety of birth and of being abandoned, just as conversely for love the primary joy is that of the erstwhile belonging to one another, the recollection of the totality so extravagantly attributed to the beloved as though it were itself all. (MARGINAL NOTE: Hate—the disappointment we discover on awakening from all-being that one cannot be all-loving.)

Yet it is possible to proceed much further in our thinking, starting with this idea of hate. Once the ego is there, with ego consciousness above, it tries once again to overcome its separation without surrendering itself. That is it tries to be at home among the things which it distributes around itself, following the principle of progressive isolation. Look clearly at the principle, however, and it turns out to be no accident at all that its origins are in the emotions born of hate and the intimation of death. In the last analysis, it consists of contrasting, taking a distance, in each and every act of perception and reasoning. To take notice of something with the senses and intellect, really means not to say "I" to it and hardly to say "You" but to set it apart for itself. When a person is concerned with those manifestations of life which remind him strongly of himself, this alienation is increased by speaking of "soul" or "mind" whereby he always means himself. In the case of events with a less familiar note, he still has recourse to the intermediate concept of "life." But when it is a matter of the "inorganic" he plainly reveals his method of cognition to be fundamentally one which strips away soul and body and mechanizes—that is a method of negative characterization. People always call anthropomorphizing the threshold of knowledge, but only *because* knowledge is so much for us a process of negation and denial. We construct only the *explicable* "material" world by means of it. It is one and the same thing to anthropomorphize and to affirm, and it is done wherever we do not explain but love, i.e., rediscover ourselves.

It is an inevitable conclusion that the whole world of material data be superordinate to the inner spiritual conceptual power with which we identify ourselves. This we express by representing the material world, intellectually and perceptually, as separated from us, in accord with the principle of isolation which divides and makes negative judgments. But once it is established, the whole thing is turned upside down in our evaluation of reality. Since the material world is that of which practical reality is constituted—exacting of us, in order to comprehend it, that we do not merely have a vivid experience of our private selves, but even may make a negative estimate of ourselves—it becomes for us automatically the prior and unconditioned reality which we assume as the basis of everything. It extends all the way to our

own physical organization, since we come to know our bodies
initially from outside like any other external object. Hence in
the end we subject ourselves to the same analytic inspection, and
inquire at which point of the series we came to life and were in-
serted as "soul" or "mind," i.e., with those very qualities we take
to be identical with ourselves, and so on. We have thus come, in
accordance with the original principle of "hate" or alienation,
to thrust ourselves from ourselves, to take a distance from ourselves. Even when we realize that we are one with ourselves
in this present moment of our current experience, we still have
excluded the past from it and only attempt to locate vestiges of it
outside ourselves, tracing ourselves in the organismic series and
arranging that series with the final result that it "rises to our
level." With everything living that we try to comprehend in accordance with its "developmental history," we coddle and pamper
ourselves tenderly back all the way from our tiny beginnings to
our present existence. For all our analytic and negating methods
we still want to find our own place in the world we thus know
and rule, i.e., to find a home somewhere to accommodate our love
and our unity despite the ego's separation.

And it is just here where psychoanalysis may be of assistance in
a new way, for in a sense it is analysis which includes everything
again within the unconscious; that sole realm gushing forth with
life unites us with our past, not only with our *own* past, and
despite the rational order we set up externally, restores us to the
uninterrupted primal order of existence.

FEBRUARY 12-13, 1913

Wednesday Discussion: Critique of Putnam[69]*—Freud and Tausk*

Sunday, February 9, after my third visit to Freud and also Monday after I got home late from a visit to Marie von Ebner-Eschenbach,[70] Tausk worked at my place on his critique of Putnam and on his second lecture on anxiety for the course.

Wednesday during the session on critical reviews the critique of Putnam burst out with the sound of drums and trumpets. Freud took the floor from Tausk and that was a signal to the others that they did not miss. I liked Tausk's behavior. At night after he returned from the Zita Hotel to the Ronacher Café he gave Federn a piece of his mind. But other gossip was noised about that he boasts of having Freud's private agreement with the critique. I had myself heard the correct wording of this remark of Freud's. Somebody is twisting everything.

Thursday I was again at Freud's for supper. Earlier in the living room he turned the conversation to Tausk and we talked a lot about him; the same later in his study and it was nearly half past one when he took me home.

There is no doubt about it that Freud acts with complete conviction when he proceeds so sharply against Tausk. But along with this "psychoanalytic" fact (that is, bearing in mind Tausk's original neurotic disposition), it is also clear that any independence around Freud, especially when it is marked by aggression and display of temperament, worries him and wounds him quite automatically in his noble egoism as investigator, forcing him to premature discussion, and so forth. The value to analysis of an independent mind can only be established in the future, and that must result in probably unavoidable battles of the present. Certain it is that for Freud it is all an annoyance and that he longs in his heart for the peace of undisturbed research which he enjoyed until 1905—until the founding of his school. And who would not wish that he might have that peace forever and ever!

So I understand very well indeed that men of intelligence and ability like Otto Rank, who is a son and nothing but a son, represent for Freud something far more to be desired. He says of Rank: "Why is it that there can't be six such charming men in our group instead of only one?" Even in his wish for a half-dozen the individuality of the man referred to is put in some doubt. And yet just this serves to reassure Freud in the face of threatening "ambivalence." During one evening's discussion when Rank lectured on regicide, Freud wrote the following note to me on a piece of paper: "R disposes of the negative aspect of his filial love by means of this interest in the psychology of regicide; that is why he is so devoted."

Discussions on Masturbation—Female and Male

Besides Freud's introduction, Ferenczi's and Reitler's statements appeal the most to me. Tausk is not at all himself in this paper but seems paralyzed.

In addition to the special temptation to excess, the harm of masturbation consists in the effort to obtain the fantasy needed to take the place of a partner. I have discovered this effort is most taxing in women with a masculine tie to the clitoris, an attitude so distant from the situation in reality, very often severe hysteria. But even in the instances when the fantasy is feminine in structure, I consider masturbation in women to be more injurious. Woman, who is the receiving one, needs close bodily contact—not only locally—much more than man. For her it is more the gift received than the gift given which in masturbating she must create by fantasying herself the partner.

This is consonant with the fact that for woman the sexual act is far more inseparably unified with her physical and psychic being. Consequently the experience continues to accompany her in its aftermath as well as in all the little details that men often know nothing about. Only woman in all likelihood knows just what it means to "cuddle," from merely resting beside each other to going to sleep together. And there is a great distinction between those lovers who are only able to excite each other and those who find peace in each other. Sexuality exists as a threat to the autonomous life of the ego, or to its daily performance in society, only in the first one-sided instance; in the second case the night of love ministers to the day and provides redoubled energy to every task that is undertaken. A man who has never known such peace, such an access of energy, can *do naught else than* despise woman or idealize her—depending on whether the ego instinct or the sexual has the upper hand. His spiritual life will become thin and lifelessly abstract, his sexuality impoverished and crude. Hence it is that basically only a man can be either ascetic or depraved; woman (whose spirit is sex, whose sex is spirit) can approach such states only to the extent that she defeminizes herself.

FEBRUARY 15, 1913

Lecture: Bisexuality—Neuroses and Sexuality—Interpretation of Dreams

Rather tired after Eysoldt's[71] matinee, the dress rehearsal of Wedekind's "Pandora's Box," with Beer-Hofmann, Schnitzler, Wassermann, and others. And also a visit from Swoboda during the afternoon, when he tried to present to me his current views on the interpretation of dreams, as seen in connection with Freud's view. Not able to make many notes on this lecture.

One of Freud's remarks dealt with Swoboda and Fliess; for

Fliess the male–female idea is so conceived that the opposite sex is always contained in the unconscious. In fact the boundaries are very blurred, and the opposite sex is just as likely to be found within the confines of consciousness as well.

He spoke very sympathetically of the enrichment which can be attained by *bi*sexuality and the extent to which it need not disturb normal development. Only when it has already become abnormal does the neurosis take charge of the situation and batten on it mightily.

Further: sexuality is always to be found as the fundamental cause of neuroses, and substitute formation is always sexual. But people generally underestimate the extent to which such a disturbance may extend to other spheres, e.g., to the ego's. Here there seems to be expressed an interpretation like Tausk's but what follows is put more emphatically. Both spheres are as one, where neuroses arise, in the realm of narcissism, without any "whence" or "whither."

Freud's final comment: since sexuality is present in the dream and in the unconscious, in general, in an indeterminate and as it were unspecialized form, it can thus come about that nonsexual things make a highly sexual appearance, and sexual things to the contrary remain unrecognized as such. This constitutes something of an innovation in the face of the *Interpretation of Dreams* (even with respect to its latest edition). And does it not seem a rather far reaching innovation with regard to the practice of dream analysis—if the latter can no longer rely on the symbol to disclose the adequate latent content?

Movies

The discussion on the evening of February 19, was devoted to Dr. Weiss's[72] lecture on rhyme and refrain which Freud praised rather half-heartedly and about which he had not much else to say. The next-to-last lecture on Saturday, February 22, was omitted on account of the exhibition of photographs of the latest Roman excavations. Tausk and his boys and I indulged in a more-or-less kindred pleasure at the Urania Theater. The movies really play a role of no small significance for us and this is not the first time I have thought about this fact. A few purely psychological considerations deserve to be added to the many things that might be said in vindication of this Cinderella of aesthetic criticism. One has to do with the fact that only the technique of the film permits the rapid sequence of pictures which approximates our own imaginative faculty; it might even be said to imitate its erratic ways. Part of the weariness to which we finally succumb in seeing works of art performed in the theater results not on account of the effort nobly expended in artistic enjoyment, but because we tire of making allowances for the clumsy way in which the illusion of movement is represented on the stage. Spared this effort in the movies we are free to bestow the mass of our uninhibited devotion to the illusion. The second consideration has to do with the fact that even though the most superficial pleasure is involved, we are presented with an extraordinarily abundant variety of forms, pictures, and impressions. Only the film is in itself able to provide some faint trace of artistic experience for both the workman in the stultifying monotony of his daily work and the intellectual worker bound to his vocational or mental treadmill. Still the two thoughts make us ponder whether this consideration for our mental state might not mean the future of the film in the theater, the little golden slipper for the Cinderella of art. Here in Vienna it was Tausk who took me to the movies despite work, weariness, and lack of time. Often we can spare only a half hour, and I always have to laugh at this activity in which we indulge.

Inversion

Tausk was full of good ideas on the theme of sex and the ego, but as we took down our notes in the evening at my place, we started at the wrong end and soon we came to a stop. Now that he is gone it is clear to me why. For to say that homosexuality is totally repressed and heterosexuality repressed only with respect to the incestuous object is to speak of two different objects in the same person. Only in the first case must it come once more to life in the transferences, full of conflict: the man comes to life in the father, the woman in the mother. In the second case, on account of the discovery of the sex difference, the primary images of the parents are something new, deepening and humanizing, so that the happiness of childhood can be added to that of maturity.

But what interests me is this: that through the establishment of the sex difference and through sexual maturation the *ego instinct as such has already been established too*—that the property of sexuality to dissolve boundaries rests on this very orientation of the boundary. Only when an ego has developed is it possible to speak of "sexuality" in a strict sense. A heterosexual person need not be anxious lest any contradiction arise between the two; rather does each benefit the other as they are contoured physiognomically each to the other.

If on the other hand the invert should be afraid of his instinctual drive it might be not only on account of its prohibited nature but also because in *his* case sexuality might exercise a destructive influence on the ego instinct; it reaches a phase of the ego which is poorly oriented and immature, although accentuated. Sexuality thrusts on him a form of sexual life which is unadapted to his primitive ego since it is derived from a later developmental period, fully directed toward objects. That perhaps is why homosexuals show a much greater inclination toward "platonic" love, and all varieties of romantic enthusiasm, particularly if they are masochistically directed. Perhaps they feel rightly that an aberration or disorder of the drive exists, even though robust souls may endure it without danger like any other injury. An especial degree of "sublimation" is needed to substitute, as it were, for its earlier but interrupted elaboration into the ego and the mental life.

No doubt our homosexual phase is in the natural course of events elaborated into a general benevolence, sociability, kindness, and so forth, and only by deviating into a special form of sexuality disturbs the development of a later phase of the ego. It is Freud's great discovery to have found a link between the seemingly asexual bond among men and homosexuality. Yet I always have the feeling that he grants an unnecessarily large role to "repression." In itself the transition from the physical to the spiritual feeling of unity with one's kind, is no more difficult than the cathectic transition from the erogenous to the genital zones. It is going too far to understand kindness as merely a reaction and hence a manifestation of repression (although it is correct to attribute *over*kindness to repressed sadism) and to base civilized man on the homosexually repressed savage. The savage, within the smaller circle of his environment, probably shows far more sociability than we do—and animals like bees and ants really do put us to shame in this respect. In animals and primitives this corresponds to the persistent "narcissistic identity"; in us it is the ground of our "sublimation" (the infantilism which never attained normal sexual maturity, it is the basis of the ego as well as of sex, wherein probably lies the true power of sublimation). Reactive qualities it is true grow higher, being revolutionary reversals of ego and sex—but still growing mostly out of the sadomasochistic confusion of the two.

FEBRUARY 23, 1913

At Freud's: Freud and Philosophy

Sunday at Freud's he told me a "fantasy" [73] (which he has not yet put down in writing and which I therefore shall not write down either) about the meaning of parricide for the development of civilization from its beginning until now. He has never before worked out anything quite so ingenious—almost more ingenious than he usually permits himself to be.

Afterward we spoke about his resistance to pure philosophy. And about his notion that it is really essential to struggle against the need peculiar to thinkers for an ultimate unity in things, recognizing this need as the product of a profoundly anthropomorphic root and custom and, furthermore, as a possible hindrance or distraction in the detailed research of positive science. As for himself, he said he has hardly had that desire to any extent worth mentioning. Subsequently we talked about the sadness which more and more accompanies our life and experience even when fortune is favorable, about the diminution of our euphoria, and about his horror at the "Poem of Life," [74] which he must have read in Nietzsche's musical version. Might there not be a connection between the two, the diminished longing for unity and the diminished euphoria? Freud acknowledged that this striving for unity has its ultimate source in narcissism. But according to his own view that is also the source of our love for life. Where joyousness prevails, there also does the longing for unity and vice versa. But to admit that much is also to confess that our life in its depths is at one accord with it, and we could not struggle against it without choking the source of all of our individual activities as well. Our thirst for life and our thirst for thought are stilled in the depths of the same spring—which hence is inviolate, sacrosanct. Surely it is bold of the man of thought to presuppose his

unity with all things or even just to "suppose" it. But is it not
still bolder of him to live as a human being?

In fact, scientific activities, the orientating as well as the practical, objective ones, also are undertaken on behalf of man's euphoria—only by a detour from the "pleasure principle" by way
of the "reality principle" and back to pleasure—to use Freud's
words. Thus it is for him at most a displacement which is involved in this; lack of euphoria would be the only reason for our
lack of interest in philosophy (or art). If someone objects (as
Freud did) that this simply amounts to regression to the infantile way of putting questions, that may once again be a case of
confusing "primitive" with "primary." The fact that something
pursues us in some form or other from our very earliest childhood might lead only to the conclusion that it is of enormous
permanent validity; its renunciation, that there is a decline in the
fullness of life. But further I have often found that such a renunciation following the philosophical or artistic enthusiasm of
youth, betokens not only weariness but actually a kind of self-
stupefaction that results from devotion to absorbing activities of
a scientific or practical kind. A sort of repression of one's self
with the aid of resignation.

The fact that whatever we say about existence in philosophic,
religious, or artistic symbols must of necessity sound false and
distorted in any scientific or practical sense need no more mislead
us today than the distortion of dreams, which reflect existen-
tial relationships that are otherwise not recognizable. Also we do
not make clear use of the word "symbol" when it stands only
for the more primitive, as mere preliminary. It comprises a form
of thinking of no logical use; it is not just a form of not-yet-
thought but is also a different mode of thought, justified in itself. Only the elements of thought appear differently mixed:
where logic proceeds abstractly, symbolic thought permits itself
the most colorful plasticity. But where logic needs to make sharp
distinctions, laying hold of each detail, there symbolism visual-

izes wholeness instead, unencumbered by prudent concretizing. (Here in the narrower purely psychoanalytic terminology a symbol is simply that which alludes to the unutterable—symbolized out of the unconscious.)

Those visits with Marie von Ebner-Eschenbach, so dear to my heart—when we even talk about psychoanalysis. And recently some unforgettable things about her brother and his death.

MARCH 2, 1913

Sigmund Freud to Lou Andreas-Salomé

I am very sorry to have to reply to your good letter in writing—i.e., because you were not with me at the Saturday lecture. I was deprived of my fixation-point and spoke falteringly. Fortunately it was the last lecture.

You have surmised correctly that I meant something different by my inquiry on Wednesday. . . . You spoil people like me who are constantly under the temptation to complain about people, by your understanding—which while it goes beyond what was said, is a correct inference. But this should be a loud warning to us not to permit ourselves too much indulgence lest we have to endure too great a renunciation later on. But it would be more rational to act so as to enjoy the present without thinking of its inevitable consequences.

MARCH 2, 1913

With Tausk: Childhood Experiences

Wednesday (February 26) Federn on neurosis and work-inhibition. Not clarified theoretically. Freud received it well but added little.

Saturday, the first of March, was the last of Freud's lectures, a beautiful one, perhaps the best of my entire winter here, and being feverish and in bed I had to miss it.

Then I got Freud's sweet letter continuing a little correspondence in the form of notes passed during Wednesday's lecture.

Sunday, Tausk's little boys came along with him as I could not yet go outside. Note: what a particular pleasure and not just a personal one, it gives me to see him and the boys together. On these Sunday afternoons everything is crowded in among the three of them, indulgence and severity alike, which under usual circumstances is spread out over the course of every day, and it is reinforced thereby. Unexpressed abundance of the past and future days is gathered together in the transitory and present moment.

We talked about the danger and necessity of prohibitions. Tausk said primary repression results as a rule only from violence toward the child through rules or punishments. Hence repressions always go back to the infantile state. If later repressions arise on other occasions without having these ancient precursors in the unconscious, they do not persist there but remain capable of becoming conscious, although they are the very repressions that are likely to be successful.

From his childhood experiences: Tausk told us how he helped himself when his mother punished him severely, silently answering her scolding epithets—"That's just what *you* are, *you* are!" —and how, finally, it came to be an automatic reactive discharge that pacified him, until one day it slipped from his lips like an uncontrolled act and stood there, alien and unintelligible to him.

And further how in an unbridled rage that demanded action, he went to the room where there was a picture of his mother in her youth and pierced it through the heart with a needle—so that for a long time he hardly dared enter the room, as if it were the scene of an actual murder. Later his mother made mention of the "scratched" picture and he was astonished until he was able to convince himself that it really was only scratched, the penetrating thrust having been made only mentally.

Later postscript: During our stay at the Munich Congress, Freud told a charming tale about his youngest son (the architect). How the tiny little fellow looked back to the sea from the stage-coach as the family was leaving Italy and declared over and over again all the while the coach was carrying him away: "I'm staying here, I'm staying here, I'm staying here!" Only when a bend in the road hid the sea from his sight did he realize his helplessness, and now pale and quiet murmured countless times, "Good-by sea, good-by sea, good-by sea!"

Fräulein E's little childhood memory, which she held to be of very little account, really contains her whole personality. On one of her birthdays (which, being only one of many in her numerous family, received little notice) she got some pretty dolls from a relative. She was very happy and pleased with them. Her only impulse, however, was to grab them and quickly get out of sight with them. She wanted to be left in peace and not made the center of attention. She threw them behind a chest in a dark room. Then came grief and repentance: longing for a happiness which was there but which she *simply did not know how to place.*

MARCH 5, 1913

Wednesday Discussion: Narcissism

Helene Stöcker[75] came as a guest. Reik[76] on art. Schnitzler. Remarks by Freud on narcissism during the long and very lively discussion. Narcissism is to be viewed as a vestigial phenomenon and one which for the present will continue to be just that; one must avoid trying to use it as a key to open up a lot of things that still remain undisclosed.

Differentiation of narcissism from egoism and introversion.

Stubborn debate between Silberer[77] and Freud, Silberer considering neither to be adequately differentiated (which is true).

FREUD: Narcissism has a pathological effect only when it in-
hibits development—just as with homosexuality, which otherwise
has an enriching effect.

FREUD: Why the artist remains narcissistic, without any developmental inhibition as the cause—because he requires narcissism, i.e., the infantile narcissistic "omnipotence of thought," in
order to be creative.

FREUD: The artist who produces his work by means of object-
cathexes transforms himself for his work's sake into all manner of
object-cathexes, something he would not do for other persons. It
is his way of loving.

TAUSK: He is not incapable of loving people; in fact his love is
beautiful, often more intense than others', and given with full
devotion but for a brief duration.

FREUD: As when women love, he constantly solicits new objects so that he may merge the world with himself; and is hence
thirsty for love's requital and embittered without it.

All this seems to me to be practically a confusion of narcissism
with its opposite; the insecurity of self-doubting, which alone
depends for its maturation on the reaction of the external world.
The erotic defect of the narcissistic person lies precisely in that
his own love's outburst nearly suffices for him. It is contact
enough for him with the world that he expresses his love. His
gratitude to his partner does not so much mean his love has been
requited as it means that the lover had the power to teach him
what love's outburst could be.

This, however, is the warmest gratitude of all, one that lasts
longer than love itself. In it, the most egoistic and the most "self-
less" love meet as one and the same in the narcissistic person. All
genuine object love is also bound to the self as object, to com-
pensate for its unegoistic quality and hence is also dependent
on the partner's behavior.

I had to give a lot of thought to these discussions insofar as they have to do with the concept of narcissism. It is certain that the concept is employed in two ways which could surely lead to extraordinarily disturbing misunderstandings, especially in enemy hands. For one thing, it is thought of as a particular developmental stage to be transcended—just as Havelock Ellis has also defined it. But thus stated it is already twofold: first as a transition between the autoerotic and the homosexual, in early childhood; but then also as self-infatuation, making its appearance, to be sure, around the time of puberty, having already known an object but taking itself as the most desirable of all objects. In this second instance, marked by unadulterated self-conceit, it may demonstrate traits approaching the neurotic intermixture of ego instincts and sexual instincts, though it need not come to a fixation of that nature. Likewise, such a pubertal phase in particular, this "second birth," may show features which suggest not only neurotic but also creative qualities, when ego and sex appear as one in a new life.

Narcissism in its creative form is no longer just a stage to be transcended; it is rather the persistent accompaniment of all our deeper experience, always present, yet still far beyond any possibility of hewing its way from consciousness into the unconscious. In narcissism the Ucs. still exists only *en bloc*, the primordial form not simply of a foundation but of the all-inclusive. Freud is perfectly right in speaking of it, as he now does, as a limiting concept, which serves as a receptacle for what remains unsolved and not a key to its solution. Still, even so defined, it is to some extent identical with the unconscious itself (not the Ucs. system of the repressed) as it lies behind its last clearly demarcated human line.

Unquestionably this point will come to be a burning issue, and it can only be settled philosophically. It is precisely here where Adler's organ concept begins, his leap from the psychological into another realm of knowledge requiring other methods. To hold fast instead to Freud's present concept of narcissism means in effect to hold fast to psychology's right to its own media and methods no matter what. And that means to be allowed to write, with appropriate obscurity, its personal mark of X, even there where the psychic organization eludes it, instead of defecting into the alien clarity belonging to another side of existence called the "physical." It means to take seriously the principle stating that psychic and physical *stand for* each other ("represent" each other, says Tausk) but neither *determine* nor *explain* the other and hence cannot substitute for each other. Hence too, it is impossible to make any psychological meaning out of Adler's "organ feeling," which is no explanation at all, touches no greater depth, but at best would constitute a means of representation. The right to an *obscurity of its own* is very important: only the eye turned toward it can find even the tiniest ray of illumination, not the eye diverted to an alien light. So it has come to Freud, here and there; for this reason, too, the greatest emphasis must remain on the direction of discovery, and the purpose of philosophic argument would be to secure its place and its justification. In Freud's cause philosophy can and ought to be merely ancillary to practical matters; but in them it has now become essential and is no longer to be circumvented.

Finally a third and beautiful narcissism appears: alongside Narcissus who looks in love at his mirrored image (sadly, says the legend, as he must if he is under a neurotic spell), and alongside the second narcissism that does not fit the name, because here Narcissus is not mirrored but becomes—gives birth to himself—and in the symbolic language of psychoanalysis does indeed come "from the water" if only as a mere image, stands Narcissus, the discoverer of himself, the self-knower.

Tausk's Course: Compulsion Neurosis— the Meaning of Holes

The last sessions were poorly attended on account of the beginning of the vacation. At the end of the first lecture on "Anxiety" he added the following conclusion as a transition to the subject of *compulsion neuroses:* just as "phobia" (anxiety) is a façade for aggression, so "ceremonial" is a façade for phobia. Freud's understanding of the compulsion neurosis is amplified by the idea that anxiety plays the primary causal role behind the ceremonial of the compulsion neurotic. (See "Obsessive Actions and Religious Practices": ". . . since we have not yet been able to arrive at a criterion of obsessional neuroses; it probably lies very deep, although we seem to sense its presence everywhere in the manifestations of the illness." [78]) This then would be *anxiety* —but Freud says so in what follows: just as in religions defensive and protective measures are at work.

In interpreting the compulsion neurosis as a "pathological counterpart to the formation of religion," as a "private religiosity," Freud touches on something of great depth in all religion. Magic and exorcism are entirely based on the binding of anxiety caused by a threat to life, by means of an imitation or simulation of a kind of natural lawfulness which coincides with the human will. To us, with our increasingly mechanistic explanation and control of the world, it is just the apparently unaccountable that seems most interesting to us in the external world and seems the work of genius in the inner world. But for earlier humanity, living in the chaos of impressions that befell them, any salvation, anything like the divine, had to be represented by established stereotypes by which they could cooperate with events as allies. All ancient art and religion always clearly speak of the ceremonial as the refuge, the unity, the union. Sin was a break in *this*

event, not any kind of action in the tumultuous external world
where we today look for sin ("sentimentally," so they say).
Hence sin could be any minimal blunder due to mere inatten-
tion—just as a wrong gesture or an unbarred bolt might be the
occasion of material disasters in the technical world of today.
Sin was then still connected with *reality* and not artificially isolated from its consequences.

Tausk was at his best in his lectures a couple of times when,
quite unruffled, he exhibited his poor memory. (When he did not
recall the name of the Spanish mountains he said: "In those—
well, those wretched mountains you know—" and when he actually could not name the five senses "—which you all know
perfectly well.") If on the other hand someone is equipped with
an exceptional memory, he has to handle his bit of knowledge so
effortlessly that one forgets it really is knowledge; where one
would emphasize his lapses, the other must discreetly hide the
wealth of knowledge. Otherwise one would be too ready to cavil
that personal effectiveness is based on power of the memory: he
accomplishes more when he acts as if he were advancing with
undecided step and not standing on a firm footing.

It is possible to establish something analogous in quite different
spheres; all gaps of this kind have the power to enhance one's
personal impression (to such an extent are we indeterminate and
undefined in our inmost self), and any of our positive mental
properties can endanger the impression as soon as they give rise
to the suspicion that they are intended to substitute for, enhance,
or make specific that which is indefinable. Gaps serve best as
holes through which we can look into the infinite. (This is appropriate in Tausk's case since they are so often caused by his
inner excitement.) Elsewhere too they are significant. Our few
senses construct a world that is not only circumscribed but that
also requires the presence of great lacunae (just as children can
only make buildings by putting blocks just so one atop the other)
—while, on the other hand, there are creatures around us (like

those species of ants which can "see" the ultraviolet) that would avoid these lacunae or set them aside. We hence depend on lacunae, which are illusory things, as if they were actual building stones possessing objective validity; here too the main thing is the infinite everywhere shining through and *making a world of it all*. Rather like the all-enveloping air in an impressionist picture. (The mark of man is to be found where humility and greatness appear to us as one.)

MARCH 12-14, 1913

Psychoanalysis and Developmental Theory

In the afternoon after Tausk had finished the lecture on "The Father Problem" in great haste, we drove to the meeting. I went on ahead and walked with Freud, who was waiting for me in the street. He was restless (on account of the closeness of the ideas to his own), questioned me during the lecture, passing a note to me: "Does he know all about it already?" I wrote back: "Of course not, nothing at all!" referring to Freud's remarks to me. He rejected him because the paper was deficient in the application of psychoanalysis to neuroses (which in fact had been studiously excluded) and because Tausk's recourse to Bachofen's views on matriarchy had made the interpretations one sided.

Invited to Freud's Friday evening. Before supper, and then again later, Freud talked readily and at length about the Tausk problem. At the end he spoke kindly and tenderly. He kept me a long time, and it was one o'clock when he began reading to me and discussing his newly concluded work for *Scientia*.[79] It is a résumé of possible scientific and practical applications of psychoanalysis. Home with him at two thirty in the morning.

I often think that if philosophical theory is not to be allowed any say in psychoanalysis directly, then it is necessary likewise to exclude more thoroughly the influence of developmental theory, as for example it is represented by Haeckel's dogmatism, than we do from our genetic point of view. But since therapy and morbid complexes are involved, the conscious state is forthwith denominated the "higher," in contrast to the "primitive" or "atavistic." These practical considerations irreparably acquire philosophic status and a fixed overemphasis on consciousness, as though everything infantile were pathological because of immaturity. It ought instead to be the task of psychoanalysis by means of its radical mode of thought to direct developmental theory (or what passes for it) beyond itself. That which we have come to understand ontogenetically in psychoanalysis in fact extends beyond that which we have constructed phylogenetically, with a certain degree of probability, and has a far wider meaning than that an event "originated" thus and so. It grasps at the roots of being itself and the roots too are of "us." The sharply ascending line of consciousness loses some of its significance on considering the all-enclosing ring of the unconscious, infinitely rounded at all points and in its omnipresence without "above" or "below." Not only what we call infantile, and hence pathological in the sense of fixation and regression, is comprised in it forever, but also what we call more simply "childlike," meaning the perpetually primordial and hence creative—without which life itself has no life. If the neuroses on account of the insight we gain in curing them lead us to overvalue the conscious state, they certainly should lead us also to emphasize the unconscious in its not only genetic significance. The fixations of the neuroses are not in themselves bad in that they imply regression, but because they do not go far enough. They get jammed on the way taking *any final stage whatever for the goal* before they have come back to the homeland of creative possibilities. So elements of the past are immersed in a violent ferment which might otherwise bear fruit for them in the future. Neurotics, however, have a notion, a feeling, of all this; they bring us news, although distorted and

misunderstood, out of the depths of our dreaming world, and
that is why they appear to us at once madder and more knowing than the unequivocally healthy. Psychotics and the most seriously insane of all do so most impressively, as Jung has beautifully
put it: they suffer from the reminiscences of mankind. They
are fixated beyond the points of individual experiences in the
truth that once had creative power, yet without reaching by this
detour over the millennia to their own creative origin, natural to
the healthy man, that is, to the person granted the economy of the
shortest route. (MARGINAL NOTE: The most creative person would
create each hour anew out of the primal abyss.)

Individualization and Reunion

Tausk's concept of the components of anxiety has been
fully anticipated in Freud's interpretation of guilt feeling. The
crux of the matter is that—quite apart from any genetic or his-
toric explanation—the father-conflict, like beholding the father,
has been a timeless experience of mankind for the very reason that
it is at the same time of ourselves and yet beyond us. It is this
fact that causes God to be present in the father, or, to put it otherwise, permits the need for God to be realized in the person of
our father. In actual human experience, the all-embracing state
wherein self and external world flow together (security and
emancipation, dependence and sovereignty) had of necessity to
fall apart into ambivalent attitudes. It was bound to become the
point of departure for all human conflicts.

Nay, it may be that here we touch on the deepest problem of
all humanity: man wants consciously to isolate himself, to take an
opposing stand. Here lies the point of his separation and also the
umbilical cord that binds him forever. Animals reach neither
this degree of independence nor this unheard-of need for reunion.

The Commonplace—Man and Woman

In the evening, when we happened to be talking about "minds of discoverers," Tausk made a very enlightening remark. Among other things it was that our knowledge of physical nature, in contrast to psychical nature, has a kind of end in itself, i.e., that we cannot go beyond it in our thinking, but can only find new facts, i.e., endeavor to make new discoveries. In the psychical world however each point is the nexus of ever-new relationships, every single new datum is at the center of the whole.

A comparable observation arose in quite a different context in our evening's colloquy. How nicely Tausk put it: commonplaceness comes not only from lack of spirit but far more from lack of life. It is simply that which can no longer germinate, but little by little wears out and becomes banal, even though it may still be clever. Hence all negative attitudes toward life, however well-founded, however ingeniously got up, lead to platitude. On the other hand, characteristic for all affirmation of life is great depth of feeling, the depth of the uncontrollable made manifest out of immeasurable interconnections. So Nietzsche says: "All pleasure wants eternity, wants deep, deep eternity" regardless how our objective psychological point of view may anatomize the concept of pleasure. The essential thing—as we agreed after a short debate—is that here we are taking cognizance of life in its wholeness as we ourselves in the fullness of life represent it, whereas life-denial is associated with a deficient experience of vitality, of which *Weltschmerz* is a symptom. Tausk's own example from during his Gymnasium years: how he arrived at his criticism of the idea of God seemingly by legitimate and objective methods but secretly motivated to it by displacement from his father, who remains inviolate like life itself. So the criticism of life, although it may be stated quite scientifically, is a symptom of a sickness, there where we live and move and have our being. We are identical with it, and however we may confront it in thought and practice, taking its measure, still in moments of real intuition when we are alive, insightful, constructive, we can only once more affirm it, just then when we are unprejudiced, unduped by our own inertia. The nonintuitive apprehension of life, which is more accessible to our intellect, does give rise to the proposition that culture has caused a decline of life, a culture obtained by a deficit in life, a culture of the weak.

In this case it would be the male sex. Men would be the weaker sex as seen from the position of woman, who is narcissistic and cultureless, woman who perhaps never attains the final insights of the mind but instead finds her being in the intuitive knowledge of life and mind.

Woman—the fortunate animal: really just as prone to regressive narcissism as the neurotic, not really undifferentiated like animals, but a regressive without a neurosis. For a neurotic, the wish to become a woman would really mean the wish to become healthy. And it is always a wish to be happy. Only in womankind is sexuality no surrender of the ego boundary, no schism; it abides as the homeland of personality, which can still include all the sublimations of the spirit without losing itself. "So do thou give as giveth a woman who loves. The fruits of her giving abide in her bosom."

Forepleasure and Endpleasure

Yesterday I further discussed with Tausk how it struck me as methodologically untidy that we describe forepleasure in psychological terms, but endpleasure in purely physiological terms, which are totally irrelevant to this climactic point of psychic life. Especially when the emotional release is strong, the end of the sexual act either dissolves the mind almost to the point of unconsciousness or else ignores it as irrelevant; conversely the greater the feeling of affection the less it requires the cooperation of the body, and the greatest affection would also be the least demanding, since it could turn the slightest physical expression to speak for the fullness of its inspiration.

Affection itself is a boundary concept, as Tausk rightly said, and in occupying a precinct at the limit of consciousness it is hence to be grasped and described consciously only at this limit. In the act itself it fully escapes us into the "lower" organic world or ascends above us, i.e., it fails to attain consciousness or it dissolves it. The portrayal of lower and upper stages comes to a stop, no more are they to be understood as affection but as organic or metaphysical representations.

We come up once more against the fact that the physical representation of our affection enters at a point where we can no longer follow it of ourselves, our feeling being bounded by consciousness. A higher symbol, as it were, it contains more than our orbit can reach; and so it is with all the final transcendental mysteries of love. However, once stated as its physical representation, it again becomes imaginable as the crude underlying stratum for everything that is still submental—out of the common origins of our ignorance.

I once more see the purpose of metaphysical expressions, and I see we still need to use them *descriptively*, untroubled by their earlier meanings. Otherwise we come to lack letters for our mental alphabet from a certain point on (more than that they would not have to be, just an X).

Baroque

Tausk recently told me something remarkable: how after times of strong intellectual productivity, forcibly terminated by outer and inner distractions, he would spontaneously develop an oversensitivity to certain forms and lines. He could stare at the movement of a horse on the street or interpret an S-shaped ornament on the table leg as if they suggested a whole world of inner relationships; it was as if he were experiencing at one and the same time all the steps that led to these formal phenomena of existence and that had been poured into them, finding in them total and boundless fulfillment.

This is no doubt characteristic of certain talented people for whom logical thought, even the most logical, is only a means, a way toward comprehensive and living knowledge. When it is unable to proceed further in its usual fashion on account of one or another kind of obstacle, it explodes at the touch of the shapes of things put before us in reality, so that they reveal their own eloquence, the wealth of their internal relations, and "the stones speak."

The very same kind of talent may on the other hand strive for the expression of an architecture of thought, for the structure and expansion of that which otherwise would remain unarticulated in feeling or action. Yet within this architecture it will easily endanger the unity of style, because of the constantly renewed irruptions and protestations of the life that again and again seeks shelter within it. The classical and logical line will often be dissolved into the baroque, for the baroque is nothing but the classical deprived of its purity by the pressure of vital impulses, the never-ending wealth of living possibility that at once destroys and builds. The baroque has been developed as a special artistic style to this end; but it is certain that a talent capable of producing it intellectually will never be expressed most productively in pure art as such, but in the unity of art and thought, thought and life.

Considered in the light of the history of art the baroque won both its glory and its odium through the growing artificiality of the material, which Renaissance art still served so honestly. One must not forget however that the baroque makes its ma-

terial available for great dreams of architecture, which would
never have come to fruition if the most precious and genuine ma-
terials had been faithfully adhered to. (There is really a kind of
analogy here with the way in which logic has been torn apart by
the inner ideational schemes that have reached out beyond logic).
It is characteristic that art became baroque with the rise of courtliness and as "princes became teachers" (seventeenth century)
with that kind of centralization and socialization of culture. The
man whose disposition is baroque wants to be effective and to
celebrate something or someone. He is no impartial isolate. The
decline of these times came when sociability and courtliness
centering around woman (France) got the upper hand. With this
feminization, ultimately every idea was permitted to be enter-
tained and boldly stated, so that one almost sees the brutal reality
of the revolution bursting forth from the same daring ideas which
were at play here.

Perversions

In the *Three Essays on Sexuality* Freud has said beautifully
in a truly medical phrase: "It is perhaps in connection precisely
with the most repulsive perversions . . . a piece of mental work
has been performed, which in spite of its horrifying result, is
the equivalent of an idealization of the instinct." [80] It is worth
reflecting that perversions, however unappealing many of them
are, are stopping places situated very close to the road to libidinal
sublimation. Indeed, the capacity of the drive for displacement
which alone makes sublimations possible, often also makes it susceptible to perversion; whereas object-love (especially the old-
fashioned "true" love of popular speech) is hard to move from its
position and, in pursuit of the sexual goal, as though placed by a
nice warm stove, gradually surrenders all mobility.

Still there is one reason why again and again object-love is regularly given incomparable preference over the perversions, and that is the fact that it alone takes us out of ourselves into reality. Our sexuality has no more important task than this, to unite us with the real world by the bridge of our physical nature. For, it is not only the marriage of one person with another but means far more than that. *Persons* represent to us more than we ourselves do the external world which we are able to live in and take into ourselves, and we only touch on the all-existent—the being of all things—by a backward turn. Only in personal relations do we find direction and rescue, whence it no doubt comes to be that ordinary object-love has won such high esteem and whence it also may be that the perversions get their peculiar and sinister horror. It certainly does not arise from mere morality. It arises from their deficient contact with reality, for which even the most sublime fantasies are of course no substitute. Perverse caresses, subtle or coarse though they may be, by preference consist of playful manipulations of the body, in heaven knows what kind of combinations, totally unadapted to the body, which is so faithfully adherent to function. It is as if such caresses slipped in secret not merely over the borders of love, but over the borders of the world with fumbling fingers vainly in quest of a hold and gliding away into somewhere—into nothingness.

Discussed with Tausk how the erogenous zones in the course of development enter the service of the ego, how for example the activity of the sensory apparatus spontaneously makes for sublimation. Now I understood this point much more clearly than ever before. Even more, while it casts light here on the original home of all sublimations, it also makes clear that the dangers and irritations which may play their roles between ego instinct and sexuality here come to a natural rendezvous. On the one hand, the ego, with the abundant vitality put at its disposal by the libido, may in its fervor rise to the level of art, to miracles of intuition; on the other hand, sexual wishes and visions may succeed in establishing their contentions when they only seem, and hesitat-

ingly at that, to intrude on the sexual sphere. They get very near
to the perversions; yet that name must be limited for serious usage to those instances when genital sexuality is abandoned for a
substitute of that sort. Under the latter conditions the ego and
sexual instincts, being already in a state of utter confusion, mu-
tually abuse one another's jurisdictions. Sadomasochism is the
clearest instance and can be called the classical case of perversion. In sadism the ego's aggression, affixing itself to sexuality,
attains a purely voluptuous satisfaction in hurting the partner,
and in masochism, conversely, the ego surrenders its rights to the
encroachments of sex. Tausk's also was the most plausible genetic
explanation of sadomasochism that I have heard: that it derives
from a period in childhood when sexual endpleasure was not yet
attainable, and a child is fixated in the forepleasure of fighting,
attack, and defeat, which comes closest to the goal. (MARGINAL
NOTE: Even without fighting, an ever increasing intensity of
stimulation equals pain.) Herein lies the motivation for the tendency to go ever further with both the infliction and the suffering of pain.

Infidelity

Tausk said once in conversation that a woman's capacity to
be psychically wedded to many things is an elaboration (sublimation) of polyandry. (Maybe the absence of jealousy is also
the result of an inability to comprehend a lasting tie of one's
own.) Two peculiarities can be often observed in this connection: first that people who are not "faithful" do not necessarily
desert one person for another, but are often simply driven *home
to themselves* and only then may make their way back to mankind again as though from a free universe. Their infidelity is
hence no betrayal. Secondly it need not be a gesture of aban-
donment for them to set free the person to whom they have

clung; more likely it is a gesture of reverence, returning him to the world. It does not reject him for being too limited or inadequate but instead engages him once more within the infinite context of relationships which close behind him and receive him into their grandeur.

A third and special consideration remains to be mentioned. A woman has no other choice than to be unfaithful or to be only half herself. In her love she is like a tree awaiting the lightning which will sunder it, but also like the tree, she desires to put forth an abundance of blooms. Since she can be the one only at the expense of the other, she needs to make the compromise of being only half herself, unless she prefers to put the whole tree in jeopardy, *but then once more plant the whole tree starting with the seed, sinking it deep into the soil.* Let it not be taken for arrogance that she requires a new beginning again and again: is it not humility to burden herself with the tiny seedling (so far removed from all the trees and the creatures of spring around it, beginning its life in the grave), instead of enduring in perpetuity, a tree shattered by the bolt?

And fourthly, there ought to be added: only when the world of fact is renounced, only when a specious existence has arisen in its place, is it *permitted* to say: "But stay!" And even more so: "Thou art so fair!" Then the feeling goes far beyond all commonplace fidelity, then all future objects are blessed and compensated for their mortality.

I have often had the occasion to make this observation: the quality in a person that delights us and the quality which later alienates us come together in the form of a whole and always as a symbol. A gesture may tell the tale, or the walk, the line of the neck, the gaze, the cadence of the voice, or even something yet more external; whatever it is, it always seems to tell all. It is an expression of the particular *contour* of the being in general, the physiognomic characteristic of him alone, and at the same time it reveals the particular private limitation of his being, from which we will eventually discover his finitude.

As long as we still believe ourselves to be faithful—and everyone does so for a while, for who has not at first imagined himself to be a paragon of nobility?—we may often perceive such traits which we suspect will limit our liking; but we still consider them harmless, just as a head cold does not bring a healthy man to think straightway of pneumonia. Later it is a more sinister matter; it can come to pass that a person at the very height of passion being fearful lest he be undone by it, may search for those tiny treacherous loopholes that may even then permit him to escape and find the freedom that beckons behind them. At last the fear is given up and, although with mixed feelings, one gets to tolerate the presence of little unsympathetic traits in the midst of the sympathetic ones, just as one comes to accept the knowledge of death. It is advancing sometime or other to us and also to our love, but we shall not on that account be constantly taking its pulse or our own. On the contrary we shall take care to turn every beat to our advantage.

Erotic life as a whole contains all of sexuality symbolically in itself, so that physical union is an absolute symbol of spiritual union, particularly in the case of woman who unites opposites more completely in her own more integrated being. One ought not forget, however, that for this very reason a man as a person cannot limit her: he too will some time become an image of unities that lie beyond him.

If you make a hole in a sandpile, no matter how deep you dig, the displaced grains of sand trickle back through the opening until the hole is filled. But, the particular position of the grains of sand relative to one another is thereafter altered, and for the very reason that the hole does not remain a hole. And the change once made persists.

There can be no dispute that for the proper conservation of the emotions two ingredients are of uncommon usefulness: namely, ambivalence or phlegm.

Emotions that keep their reverse aspect "faced toward the unconscious" can never be turned toward us *in toto*. Hence we can never see them in their entirety. If we could, the consequence would perhaps be like what befell him who gazed on the countenance of truth in the picture at Sais:[81] he that beholds it dies.

The phlegmatic disposition, on the other hand, simply stays away from the flare-up of intensity. That which is not used intensively remains new longer.

Whoever is not at all, or very little, disposed to ambivalence, can only afford to devote himself fully to someone or something with the aid of absolutely essential interruptions by which he can turn back once more wholly to himself. Gratefully, gaily, at such times he loses sight of the emotion he has just felt instead of reluctantly and hatefully, as when ambivalence exists, never letting go. But only the former style is called "infidelity," since an unwilling fidelity is sure to make its presence known by an unremitting virtue.

Significantly, a neurotic—and hence a very ambivalent person—can be cured of a fidelity ("fixation") only if we avoid a unilateral approach to it and succeed in getting behind both sides: only then will fidelity wither on the vine of uprooted hatred.

MARCH 21, 1913

Alfred Adler

Said good-by to Adler on Good Friday at the Alserhof, having last spoken with him at the end of February, when on my account he had left the group at his house because I did not want to take part in it. It would have been all right for me to keep silent as Freud wanted; that not succeeding, we got into an argument about Freud.

Things have gone so far with Adler that as far as I am concerned I shall remember his book *Organ Inferiority* as the best of his writings. It is there that inferior organs are depicted as at the same time of persistently infantile character and as those which can develop further only postnatally and only by way of "nervousness" at that, as their overexcitability patently declares. All this is beyond the capacity of specialized and physiologically sound organs. Even today this all strikes me as an exceptionally stimulating and thought-provoking organic foundation for Freud's discoveries and at the same time in happy accord with numerous recent biological investigations on the glands and the like.

But organ feeling (in a medical sense) is outside the reach of any psychological consideration; it remains a sphere of its own and no substitute for the basis provided by Freud. Under circumstances in which the organic basis of psychic life might be demonstrable, it would not be for our eyes to see, since they would find it only the last refuge of the incomprehensible. Where we are able to behold the physical operations of mind we can observe nothing of the psyche behind it. Old-fashioned materialism of ill repute, deriving one thing from the other as cause and effect, thus becomes an intellectual blind alley; the concept of parallelism also is negated by these laborious "localizations" of psychic processes in physical ones. By completely differentiating its methods as well as its data, psychoanalysis, despite its rejection of philosophy, alone proceeds along sound philosophical lines, its apparent dualism being uniquely hospitable to a true monism. It must therefore insist that the psyche which Adler regards as if it consisted of fictional constructs, does not exist in a vacuum, but partakes of the same real meaning for practical thought (i.e., thought not engaged in epistemological problems) as the physiological substrate does for medical research. It is almost as if Adler had turned "ambivalence" (he claims to have discovered it before Bleuler), the unconscious prototypes of the psyche, and the antithetical pairs into an arbitrary and capricious multiplicity and finally into a total arbitrariness. One might make

the poor joke that he had taken the term narcissism too seriously
and literally, had gazed so long on his own reflection in it until
nothing of Narcissus was real for him but the image. When it
reached that point he based his theory of fiction, as stated in
The Neurotic Constitution on Vaihinger's[82] philosophy of
"as if." This philosophy speaks of purely auxiliary constructs of
theoretical ideas, of "arrangements" which must on two accounts
be absolutely differentiated from Adler's. In the first place they
operate on a completely conscious basis; in the second place they
exist quite beyond any value judgments (a fact on which Vaihinger
puts special stress, having, God knows, no intention of colliding
with the Kantian problem of moral values, although he is no
longer in theory an orthodox Kantian). The fictitious goals posed
by Adler's theory are the exact opposite of these, being effective
only in that they are *un*conscious and perishing when they become conscious; in addition they constitute the genuine reser-
voirs of value, invulnerable to any criticism. It is also not to be
overlooked that he does not regard the fictions as symptoms of
disorder, but as the central mental manifestations of the healthy
person, one might say as the only symptom of mental activity in
Adler's model man. Hence it is quite impossible for him to discriminate in this area between the sick and the well. The actual
distinction is founded on the fact that the healthy fiction is not one
at all. Even its most venturesome dream still originates in a reality,
denied by Adler, out of which we create our lives in an external
reality of their own. To acknowledge this would put him on the
road back to Freud. He would have to see that the soul is even
further involved in the symbolic process than he claims, just because it has something to symbolize. Positive reality, the substance of mind, only in disease deformed into empty fictions, is
represented in the mind by a sequence of images of what which
really exists and is not itself reducible to an image or a name.

APRIL 2, 1913

Wednesday Discussion—Departure

After many farewells during the past days, at the clinic and at dear old Ebner's (on March 29), now my last Wednesday.

Sachs[83] lectured amusingly on Swift, using hardly any notes. Freud was pleased. I noted down one of his comments (unrelated to Sachs's subject):

In order to state its problems psychoanalysis needs a clear demarcation of the domain of the neuroses from general psychology's as well as from Adler's. Adler's theory of inferiority, for example, unquestioningly has "social significance" for the development of character as well as experience. Important as it may be, however, for anyone to be physically handicapped, especially to be handicapped with respect to the genital, this is found to be a cause of neuroses only now and then, but neuroses are very often found when the body is intact. The fundamental causes must be grasped then in those very depths of the psyche itself in which the psychic structure originates.

As I went downstairs with Freud he invited me to come on Sunday. Turning back jokingly to those who followed us he asked gaily whether he ought not hurry up and set the stage for a little farewell party. No! But shortly before that, while I was still sitting at his side, I nearly raised my hand to ask to speak for the first time, and I would have said thus:

Gentlemen, I have not wanted to enter the debate and I have let you do it for me but I do want to express my gratitude myself. I can thank psychoanalysis that it demands more than the work of isolated scholars at their desks and hence admitted me *here* to a kind of fraternity. The source of its vitality does not lie in any hazy mixture of science and sectarianism, but in having adopted as a fundamental principle that which is the highest principle of all scientific activity. I mean honesty. It turns to this principle over and over again even in the most individual reality, and in so doing it subjects life to knowledge, just as its scientific glory is based on the fact that it has turned to life the constricted and dried-up knowledge of academic psychology. It is for this very reason that cleavages and conflicts are more likely to come to be in this group and beyond it than elsewhere, and it is harder here than elsewhere to reconcile them without endangering the coherence of the methods and the data. This will surely continue to be a problem for some time to come, but it is the stamp of a progress motivated not only intellectually but also personally, and as long as it abides by the ideal of the honest community then it is also a beautiful thing and a joy, at least in a woman's eyes, to see men opposing one another in struggle. And it is all the more my duty today to perform the other task, to give thanks. Thanks for all these evenings, even the tiresome ones, on account of the man who presided at them and devoted his time to them. And thus the tasks of the sexes in this world have been done separately and still in union. For men fight. Women give thanks.

APRIL 6, 1913

Last Visit to Freud's

Sunday, my last visit to Freud's. At tea we discussed the distinction between abnormalities (which can assume monstrous proportion) and neuroses and also how seldom it is possible to remove perversions, so that ordinarily one has to be content to come to terms with their continuing presence.

Later in his study: on the conflict between therapy and research. To be sure patients are an impressive source of material, insofar as they are the only ones who furnish the physician with his knowledge, which the internist to a certain extent obtains from dead or anesthetized bodies. He went on to say very well that it will depend on our gaining further knowledge—most abundantly enriched by incurable and unhappy cases—to make possible an ever more reliable therapy, until there might be at least as much a distinction between the practicing physician and scientific research worker as is the case now in medicine.

At the same time he put exceptionally strong emphasis on the necessity of maintaining the closest and most persistent contact with the pathological material (the difficulty with unremitting work in the unconscious realm is accounted for, I think, by the unusual novelty of the findings, which are continually opening up new doors). This great worker who has ten analytic hours in addition to his theoretical work at night, would be "satisfied" with seven to eight hours of analysis. In the long run it cannot be done in less time because psychoanalytic research is in almost the same situation as the dream, which is not preserved by concentrated association on it; it becomes irretrievably submerged. There are and will remain two worlds; one knows in one's heart that this man's strong mind is most at home in the other world, that of norms. Perhaps his work is most assuredly the work of a genius in that it is an achievement involving the other person, and only partly himself.

As I set out home with his roses, I rejoiced that I had met with him on my journey and was permitted to experience him—as the turning-point of my life.

Retrospect

When I look back on the Saturday and Wednesday discussions and Freud's articles of the last half year, it seems that he has loosened his views somewhat on five points. (1) In respect to repressed material as the unique content of the unconscious as he conceives it; (2) in respect to neuroses as a bilateral disturbance of both ego instinct and sex instinct; (3) in respect to a more intelligible implication of the ego in narcissism; (4) in leaving open the more precise definition of the term censorship; (5) in the observation that in dreams content of a latently sexual nature may acquire a nonsexual form and vice versa.

In all these points the ego has been accorded a role of greater equality with that of sexuality; there is consequently discernible an advance toward those who either have defected or threatened to do so, all except Adler. Only Adler takes the stand not of emphasizing the ego, but of eliminating the role of sex, and hence of negating the two-sidedness of the relation. But here alone lies the crux of the matter, and thus Freud is right.

II
Journeys and Meetings

With Ferenczi

The data that Ferenczi showed me all came out of his diary, and I shall make no mention here of the six papers we singled out of it. I shall only put down some observations that occurred to me later when I tried to orient myself further.

The poverty of consciousness in contrast to the extravagance of nature. The *degree* of determinateness gives the impression of freedom. The "will" equals passivity, gushing forth whenever inhibitions leave room for it, and all the more stormily when inhibition has been more confining.

One could say: the conscious like the unconscious has its own kind of homogeneity as well as its own kind of fragmentation. That which comes to the surface in the dream is so uniform in its latent state that it is undisturbed by its colorful context. Conversely, we want to establish the "material" nature of all the multiplicity of our waking percepts and call them comprehensibly "reality."

Freud's original conception was that only repressed material forms the content of the unconscious. Somewhere in his later writings, and also once in class, he departed from this view to include material which *almost* attains consciousness but is thrust out before actually entering it. In the first case one would discover in the unconscious only those mental elements which represent rudimentary ideas rather than primary elements characteristic of the unconscious itself. Even in the second case the question is at least a moot one.

But on the other hand, if Freud granted Ferenczi's reply to the question a second difficulty would ensue, namely that the essential distinction between Ucs. and the field of consciousness would appear leveled off; the upshot would be something akin to Adler's concept of layering. It would in any case be dangerous to find oneself on the same plane with Adler and the other "defectors" (even only by their misunderstanding).

We might conceptualize in the following way the repression of those thoughts which press toward consciousness without quite attaining it (those which are so to speak nipped in the bud): a tendency to repression reigns not only at the throne of consciousness but throughout all our subterranean world of becoming as well. It is that tendency which determines the natural outlines of our inner physiognomy by instinctively selecting or barring possible stimuli. Just as every living organism manifests the limitations of its own life by such rhythms in its reactions. The viability of thoughts is thus decided a priori; their subsequent repression from consciousness would be only a repetition at greater intensity of what occurs anyhow (down in the somatic depths). Thus the unconscious really contains in itself the preformed elements of all later conscious thought as well as the structure of all ideals.

In the conversations with Ferenczi it became very clear to me that all Freud's well-wishers must for the present hope for the most tolerant policy on his part toward the schisms. This policy is best for his own work and peace of mind and hence also indirectly for his cause, since in the long run even those who followed divergent paths must unwittingly prepare the way for him by referring us back to him. (Freud wants "the most undogmatic" freedom.)

But such a policy will turn out to be the most dangerous one for those who come after him. They are the ones who will have to answer for all such contradictions with their own destinies.

The trouble with ambivalence is not just that it permits hatred to permeate love. For objective relations it seems to me nearly more dangerous that in our struggle against the persistent threats of ambivalence we dare not own up to the natural and healthy limits of all relationships. Unquestionably Ferenczi has many ideas which for one thing alienate him from Freud's philosophical position. However fantastic the consequences of some of them may yet seem to Ferenczi himself, it would be good if his way of seeing things would influence Freud's philosophical views. But it is significant that Ferenczi speaks of these, his dearest ideas, those by which he might be said to live in his lonely state (as the manner of his talking about them plainly attests), as "craziness," "pathological curiosity," and his burning "desire for omniscience."

These days in Budapest have been so valuable to me following the hours I had already had in Vienna with Ferenczi, and I got much closer to him. I am passionately interested in his work and in his method of working. Perhaps publication of Ferenczi's ideas is premature with respect to Freud's present and next endeavors, but they really *are* complementary. So Ferenczi's time *must* come.

GÖTTINGEN: LOUFRIED, WHITSUN, MAY 11, 1913

Not a sound from Rainer since his winter letters, but seeing his sandals in the hall I think of the Whitsun week he spent here (years ago).

Around Whitsuntide last year was the last time I spent with B.[84] When I think of the two of them it always seems as though coming as they do from such opposite origins their paths must cross someplace midway.

Both blonde haired, with sensuous mouths, splendid brows, otherwise rather different.

Rainer's head with its receding chin and almost no occiput, rests on narrow shoulders, a thin neck. B is thick-set, short-necked, the back of his massive head almost continuous with his shoulders; accentuated jaws; the whole towerlike physiognomy can be drawn with a single line. With a bit of exaggeration the over-all impression could be put in a word: one, the sickly aristocrat, the other, the parvenu who has overextended himself.

Rainer is disposed to oversensitivity both by his heredity and his upbringing (the parents nervous people, unhappily married and separated, he himself brought up as a girl to take the place of a dead sister, then homeless and shoved around from school to school, military and others); with his genius he turned all this to creativity and reached in its discipline the greatest possible austerity. A lyric poet, he nevertheless concentrated his powers early in life and unsparingly sheared off all dilettantism and vacillation, but became totally disorganized in his personal life.

B, on the other hand, has his origins in the world of reality, even banality (a commercial family in his case, the father being the frivolous one, as in Rainer's the mother), he himself is somewhat given to the banal and brutal, which he has corrected by means of another brutality—the complete personal revolution that made him a noble "helper" and savior, but on account of his lack of inner freedom paralyzed his creative talent. He appears a many-sided man, a bit of a dilettante, determined to attain in every respect his "own" spiritual goal—to *rise*.

One is a typical hysteric, the victim of his physical condition, abandoning himself in his devotion, owned by nobody, not knowing to whom he belongs, until he comes as one delivered into the homeland of creativity. The other a no-less typical obsessional neurotic bound up in a thousand reproaches and fixations, ever too "settled," tied-up, and self-conscious even in regard to his work and his life and hence not seeking a homeland in it but instead a passage, a route, a bridge to the world. Rainer's dream: to be "a thing among things," at peace and finally integrated. And conversely B's horror when he learned of my dream in which he had become a statue and said: "I am becoming an object!" Consequently Rainer stands free among men, driven almost out of himself, capable of playing any role, happy in acting, reciting, being loved, and at the same time a passionate solitary because he can also do all these things alone by himself. B is diffident and shy with others, full of a burning ambition that he disowns. I can never forget his shrill and trembling schoolboy voice when he lectured.

Rainer longs to be a country doctor, a man of help and blessing, holy, a priest, a monk. Sometimes it is this ideal of perfection, which in practical reality is totally foreign to him, that makes a great impression on young people. B on the other hand was wildly thrilled by my father's little story in the Napoleonic manner about Nicholas I and the Decabrists: aggression, omnipotence, explosive and cruel ambition that tore to pieces all his middle class propriety.[85]

But this is what makes him unhappier than Rainer can ever be with all his attacks of desperation: that he *needs* his middle-class vocation as a physician and the halo so hardly won. However, it means a personal revolution for him, being turned upside down, and he complains that he feels indifference and not human kindness (in other words that he uses people as a means to self-abnegation and self-improvement). Yet it is the only remaining bridge for him to the external world, the only surviving surrogate for any assertion of his temperament. That goes for his love life too; even his marriage and his wife fit the pattern in an unusually frightful way, with him acting as his wife's nurse, her helper, and the savior of her life. Only thus was love allowed to him and only thus was it possible for him to have anyone at his

side, a "loneliness for two." That is how he made his self-indulgence legitimate and even then only with the understanding that it precluded any progress into the inner world as well as the outer. His seemingly delicate sexual disposition has in a way a more disturbed foundation than Rainer's, who also appears delicately constituted and yet gives of himself unrestrainedly. Rainer's deficiencies are directed externally or to the surface of his own person as abuses or weaknesses, but they are no secret to *him*. He can afford to admit all, since the hour of genius extends its grace to him on just such occasions of failure. But B cannot confess even to himself; that is what a life based on revolt presupposes. No hour of grace compensates him for all the miseries of self-dissimulation, only the enduring bond of a perfection that wearies him.

Guilt Mechanisms

Freud's discoveries have beautifully advanced our understanding of how feelings of remorse and the like are produced by prohibitions that originally had a functional basis, later forgotten, so that fear of punishment appears mystically joined to deed. It is of extraordinary significance that we can now learn from neurotics the way that feelings of guilt and anxiety which have quite another origin can attach themselves unwarrantedly to the most innocent actions. We observe the mechanism whereby this can and does happen at any time without losing its ghostly power, which we formerly thought of as slowly acquired, even as phylogenetically inherited. Now for the first time it has become untenable to object, as many did on purely emotional grounds, to the utilitarian genesis of the bite of conscience. They were right to feel that these uncanny things could flow forth from incomprehensible sources of their own, irrespective of the utilitarian aspect.

The second point about instinctual repression without any particular prohibition of one's own or someone else's, simply arising in the conflict among the manifold drives, seems to me insufficiently differentiated. Naturally when one instinct is driven out by a neighboring one or an opposite one, pain and a kind of schism result. To this extent illness and health differ only in degree. But in this pain and schism, feelings of anxiety and remorse are warded off, and conflict at the center of the personality is presented by the fact that both drive and counterdrive have the effect of amplifying life and not of restricting it. They represent the friction within the integrated personality, advancing and enriching it, because alongside the drive which succeeds the others become perceptible. The personality learns to embrace the latter too and draw them into the conscious enclave of the ego. Instead of a cleavage the result is a heightened unity of the self.

It naturally makes no difference to this end whether the egoistic instincts force out the altruistic or vice versa, although we are accustomed to confuse only the former instance with remorse. In either case, the subsequent pain merely represents the cost of success which has been permitted, a cost which has been set by nature itself, increased only in proportion to the liveliness of our ego feeling. We would best attribute its absence not to a more unified personality, but to a more rudimentary or stunted one, which is hardly able to take notice of the instinctual activity within its being, in fact still lacks or has already lost full being. To me however, the most interesting thing about all this is that all at once now qualitative relationships are reduced to quantitative ones. It is purely a question of amount, whether for example egoism itself provides instinctual gratification, or whether its hidden consequences can be expressed in the emotional life. That is, can this egoism itself tolerate repeated splitting only to reunite itself ever anew and more broadly, experiencing every death as a rebirth and every pain as a renewed stimulus to life?

So I think that just as the pathological material argues against the concept of a purely utilitarian origin of conscience—since, as Freud has demonstrated, guilt feelings may arise spontaneously —so too there are inner objections to the proposed amplification of the concept on purely pathological grounds. Even more spontaneously, our lives are always enriched by the most vital centers, where friction, conflict, polarity, ever anew make possible the creative return to the depths.

There is something about the *fear of death* that makes one think of a quite peculiar form of guilt feeling. Often it is our punishment for insufficient love of life; that is, that we have repressed too much of it and so doing have failed to keep in unity with it and ourselves. Life then took on the aspect of death, i.e., it no longer loved us, and anxiety is the manifestation of this displacement. The love of life is the only way, but the sure way to be exempt from death, for death is a prejudice.

Cruelty—Compassion

We often understand by the word cruelty something quite different. That is, we assume nothing particularly cruel in the mind of the person involved; cruelty is suggested only by the outcome. So it is when we are the cause of pain without realizing the object's capacity for pain (as children often do), when we express anger by an outburst of hatred which we turn with equal spontaneity against an inanimate object, intending its destruction for our own satisfaction and quite unconcerned whether it suffers or not.

True cruelty is a quite special mental process arising when naïve and natural mischief, savagery, and brutality, which animals employ for their vital necessities, escape from the domain of self-preservation, encroach on sexuality, and lay hold of it. Hence a terribly strange and weird quality that is the enigma of cruelty:

that it is only imposed on the beloved object and increases in proportion to the love. To show it to an indifferent person would be embarrassing, and to show it to an antipathetic one would be unbearable for the very reason that it implies a degree of intimacy which in such cases would be prostituted. I have found that persons of this kind can often and unexpectedly be detected by their close yet bashful attentiveness to manifestations of pain or to accounts of painful things. They are excited by them but certainly not eager to hear; rather it is a torment to them as if they had to eavesdrop on the sexual intimacies of strangers, which they might find disgusting.

Cruel people being always masochists also, the whole thing is inseparable from bisexuality. And that has a deep meaning. The first time I ever discussed this theme was with Nietzsche (that sadomasochist unto himself). And I know that afterward we dared not look at each other.

Compassion too can be manifold: identification from sympathy (homosexual libido); identification based on the thought that the same thing might befall oneself; identification from direct or displaced guilt feeling (e.g., excessive concern due to death wishes or oversensitivity toward all kinds of living creatures based on remorse for brutality toward one of them—reaction).

Reality

In Freud's short and most philosophical work, the "Formulations of the Two Principles of Mental Functioning," [86] he calls the *reality principle* the detour to be taken by the *pleasure principle* in order to attain its own goal. It is certain that man is always engaged in a two-sided effort: on the one hand, to unite himself to everything and all to himself (in accordance with the direct pleasure principle as described by Freud), and, on the other hand, to extend further and further the lessons learned on the "detour"—namely to divide, organize, differentiate himself and the outside world thereby created. One might entertain the idea that what we call reality, meaning the world in contrast to ourselves, is basically a compromise between these two efforts.

Indeed we forget the twofoldness of ourselves and the world every time we really give ourselves totally to ecstatic involvement with someone or something. We are sharply reminded of it once again only when it is right before us in our unappeased longing to be at one with and in all or conversely in our attempt to define every single thing more precisely and distinguish it from ourselves. Once more face to face with actual "reality," we merely substitute with our concept "real" for the undeniable totality of the universe, otherwise lost in all its distinctions and individualizations. Thus both aspects are accounted for. Of course so understood, "reality" almost would amount to a symptomatic action, not absolutely different from the projections of patients except that in this case the consensus of mankind is fully in agreement and constructs its whole practical existence on it. All the same, the obstinate way in which things continue and persevere as a result in their reality, itself might stem from the fact that it is a kind of compromise. Things stand outside, over against us, and thereby are actually in being outside us, simply because the ego's pure activity is unable to penetrate them completely and comes to a halt at some sort of boundary. The ego is therefore not itself "reality" in this sense, but rather is so thoroughly functional and living that philosophically it is put "in doubt." That which is real in the sense of being external has been left hanging halfway and paradoxically is supposed to cope with the duality.

The interpretation of reality, so called, as only appearance and illusion was closely approached by ancient wisdom, from the Hindus beyond Kant to the most modern epistemology. If these teachings have always remained esoteric and have failed to mislead our naïve judgment, that is because our naïve judgment is right notwithstanding. Right for the simple reason that the whole method of fragmentation by which we construct the multiplicity that confronts us only demonstrates our inability to follow it any further by a living identification of ourselves with it. Hence it represents something above us (above our sundered ego). It is like an array of dummy figures in which while no longer present to our immediate awareness, the essence of life is still contained, and it is always and ever the indivisible whole of it within each one. *Alles Vergängliche ist nur (s)ein Gleichnis.* It is not only to take our bearings in a practical sense that we bow to what is called external reality as the decisive factor. Philosophically speaking too, there is nothing that comes so close to the truth as *boundless reverence for all that exists.*

The process of cognition, by means of division, perception, and logic, is hence also enveloped in symbolism. It is only in fact an extension of the way we make pictures to stand for the undivided whole, making it possible at the same time to observe it further and in detail, while preserving the unity undiminished in every tiny detail, keeping it concrete even in an infinite regress of divisions. To all *appearances* this kind of activity is utterly different from what we call "symbolization." That is only because *there* we glue our eyes to the differentiated and the multiple which is accumulated in it. In so doing we split up the indivisible. Where the unconscious reveals a will to form, it is already on the road that logic follows to the end; where we make logical distinctions we are still engaged in making likenesses representing "reality," in order not to speak of God (i.e., of the essence). (For like reasons every mental illness persists in its madness in "creating reality," and the worse the illness the more so; that is it comes, roundabout from the back door, to the same result).

Sublimation

The genetic point of view is so disposed to treat the "primitive" as an obstacle to be overcome that it must at times lose sight of the enduring "primary" element. It has endowed the concept of sublimation with the perilous role of standing in opposition to the natural. Being the total expression of humanity, nature and culture are everywhere present together, but in this view the distinction is historically, i.e., artificially, intensified so that sublimation and repression are pushed into an ominous kinship. In fact, modern man as well as the "savage" accepts natural limitations—the latter no less—not just as a departure from nature but also in accord with his own real being. It is quite analogous to sexuality, which becomes procreative only when it is forced out of the realm of the erogenous zones into the genital zone. That is not sublimation, not a departure from the sexual goal, but on the contrary the attainment of the goal; likewise the subordination of nature to culture is only seemingly a denaturing process and itself takes place on the same natural foundation. We have only two ways open to us to express our central being: either by drawing the world into ourselves in our dreams or by breaking through the limits imposed on the ego by its separation from and opposition to the world and devoting ourselves to objective reality. Anyone who is creatively gifted and not pathologically inhibited at last finds anchorage in cultural activity, no matter how much narcissistic satisfaction he may seek in himself. So America was discovered when the intended goal of the journey was its opposite, the dreamland of India. Actually it is our own self-realization that we call by the name "sublimation"; Tausk's word "elaboration" is much better and has recently come into more frequent usage. It means the living application of the gifts of nature to their own purposes;

only someone who considers these purposes metaphysically and spiritualistically would be allowed to tear the two apart. (Of course it does not alter the situation at all that we are the victims of cultural atrocities and blunders, just as all natural existence suffers from its insufficiency.)

Only *that* man who like Prometheus has created culture for himself and has thus created human existence anew as a second reality is at the same time Narcissus, fully evolved, standing before his own image. It is himself he gazes on. He is not the beaten slave forced against his will to escape from himself. It is wrong to see nature and culture opposed like sunlight and shadow in respect to our natural desire for happiness and the ego's fulfillment. It is wrong to think that the increase of the shadow coincides with the slanting of the sunlight; it is a false and contrived picture. The right picture is rather that of the plant around high noon: then it casts its own shadow straight down beneath it, a self-duplication wherein it gazes on its own repeated outline, its finest safeguard from the great flame that would consume it before its fruiting.

Ambivalence

The ambivalent attitude is generally considered to be either pathological or the expression of primitive humanity, the latter particularly so since [Freud's] remarkable observations on the "antithetical sense of primal words," and the like.[87] In this ancient knowledge however there lingers an understanding only painfully arrived at by us moderns with all our knowledge. To think conclusively about the relative almost amounts to thinking of the absolute as did Spinoza. As a matter of fact, while the people of the ancient great religious cultures may not have *thought* like Spinoza, in a way they still *lived* their lives on the edge of the absolute.

The reason for this is that ambivalence is basically and inescapably rooted in all manifestations of life itself. Ambivalence is nothing but the polarity or duality which life never outgrows, and all the creative activity on which the culture of humanity rests flowers from it. Here the distinction—creative, primitive, and neurotic—cannot be clearly and distinctly drawn. The unconscious, in itself indivisible, makes itself outwardly known in the enveloping pairs of opposites. The creative act finds intelligible symbols drawn from the surface; hinder it but a little and the concrete opposites, symbolically destitute, alternately pull each other up like a seesaw. The affect involved is then like a fish that still wriggles in the water after being hooked; it can neither swim nor die.

Ambivalence in the healthy person is presumably held in check by the natural confining pattern supporting the specific physiognomy of his feelings. Paradoxically, thus his ambivalence only serves to express his integratedness.

We do not always make a sufficient distinction between ambivalence and reaction formation. In the latter case when an instinctual drive subsides following satisfaction it gives place to an opposing one. Here it is the succession that is so characteristic.

Enchantment

Psychoanalysis provides a plausible interpretation of those fairy tales in which something ugly or disgusting is transformed into something glorious (such as a frog into a prince): namely, that with the lifting of repression the sexual object is transformed by sexual love into something desired. Of course it is possible that here too sexuality has the role of symbol of symbols. This is a difficult question to decide, all the more so because in former times the sexual symbolized everything, and the limits of physical and mental were not so narrowly and strictly drawn as they are with us.

In any case, these fairy-tale enchantments lend themselves very nicely to further symbolizations. It need not be just the phallus which turns out to be a prince, when repugnance is overcome and the frog taken to bed. Far more likely rather it is as if ugliness and banality have more symbolic significance in our lives than anything else, more than greatness and splendor. The limits of our comprehension and of our sympathetic understanding are thereby marked, whence come the ugly and the banal. (Actually we could also say philosophically that, taken separately, things seem generally inadequate and meaningless because we do not experience them in their universality, their autonomy, on account of our own isolatedness. It was quite natural for early man, creator of the fairy tale, that the One could easily stand symbolically —and not only symbolically—for the All, and vice versa.) Unrecognizably disguised by banality and ugliness, an enchanted splendor might only be in hiding. When at times we surmise their presence, things that we ordinarily value not for any intrinsic worth but for ulterior purposes acquire an unwonted aura of majesty. It may come out (for repression assigns great significance to such things, although of the most untoward kind) in the unexpected violence of disgust and horror which they inspire in us when things are not well with us; behind them an understanding love is at work, but not yet come to life. These things suddenly become so unreal and frightening because of our fear that we cannot grasp their full meaning as we ought. Suddenly too all the rest of reality depends on them, just as a giant allows a man to dangle on his little finger. He can see nothing but the little finger, but the event leads us to suspect the presence of the giant. Anxiety (guilt feeling: *to be unable*) is released in a sacrificial act (the overcoming of our horror), and thereby we grasp the glorious meaning now freed of enchantment. When we overcame ourselves, i.e., liberated ourselves from repressiveness and confinement, we became at one with the meaning, which is not bound to things that have become separate and banal. This is most perspicuously apparent in the sexual symbol, for the ugly insignificant little phallus proves to be the father of worlds.

A comment by Sabina Spielrein,[88] on why a misfortune shared by all is made more bearable (pain is the consequence of the differentiation of an isolated ego representation), makes plain that the remedy lies not so much in knowing that others have been drawn into misfortune with us, but in knowing that we ourselves have been drawn out of it. No longer involved in it as utterly special beings but as parts of a universal being, we acquire a sort of schizophrenic indifference—are divorced from our most peculiarly personal quality—and in our hearts think of it more in pictures than with our present affects.

On Libido

In his critique of Jung's book on the libido,[89] Ferenczi has rightly charged Jung with attributing to Freud a change of outlook which Freud has never proposed and with a vain attempt at justifying the change by enlarging the concept of libido so far that ego and sexuality are both harmoniously accommodated in it. Still, Jung is right in claiming that the character of the libido is too narrowly construed as sexual in the interpretation given to incest, since this incest originally occurs at a time in life when one is hardly able to speak of a differentiation between subject and object. I think however that the case still less admits the term "presexual" in its specific sense, suggesting as that does an exaggeration of the egoistic drive in the need for nourishment. The two are still only one, and a mutual struggle for priority between instincts which are only later distinct is quite superfluous. Jung has clearly been led astray into his innovation not only by his proclivity to premature synthesis which he shares with others; it is also because he is the one to whom we are most indebted for the discovery of the relationship between libido regressions and archaic thought. Inasmuch as archaic thought is symbolic thought, he considers the libido itself to be symbolized in it, emerging there in its original aspect.

When we reflect on Freud's concept of the libido, altered as it has in fact been with the passage of time, it becomes exceedingly plain why he finds there the fundamental basis for all psychic life. Sexual excitement is the one way in which the organic makes itself known to us in a specifically psychical manner. Its function is in this respect not like that of the other organs as manifested in conditions of improved or deteriorated health, and in general operating to stimulate or retard. It is doubly different: first through the peculiarity of the excitement itself, producing organic effects through psychic means, and secondly in its characteristic encroachment on the psyche as a whole, including the capacity for judgment—in which it is often likened to an intoxication. In Freud's view we here behold the intersection of the physical and the psychical that permits to psychology no further backward turn.

It is here too, no doubt, that the libido has always made its strongest impression on mankind, bodily events being mysteriously raised to the level of mind and psychic events grounded in the physical. We must realize that man can never have suffered more fundamentally than in becoming a conscious human being, seeing the abyss plunging between himself and all the rest, between his race and the world, the beginnings of the inner–outer division. Everything then pertaining to the libido is like an oasis in the desert, like the raft rescuing from the flood. Here at least inner and outer were one; he and the world once more were a perfect whole. What a glory must have attended the mere satisfaction of sexual desire! How natural it was that every religious ceremony centered around the sexual act! And more solemnly than we today can even imagine in any moment of consecration of our personal love, since we know neither such brute necessity nor such deliverance from it (except in psychosis, when the

world of reality once again trembles beneath the feet). With all
our sublimations of love today the danger is far greater that we
shall lose the original religious meaning of human union in the
sexual act. We become wedded to reality in it, and the numbness
to which we are reduced through sex, when ego and world are
dissolved, is proclaimed to be external reality. This simple miracle no longer being one, we are inclined to treat sexuality as a
commonplace, or else sentimentally (romantically). Early man
too knew it as a commonplace and took it so, like animal hunger,
but he also knew the sacrificial feast which he shared with the
god.

Bleuler: Autistic Thought

In certain respects Bleuler's[90] objections to Freud can be put
differently. For example, it is true that Freud's pleasure principle
does not suffice to explain how selfhood is asserted through unpleasurable affects, but both are comprehended in a more complete assertion of life where in some cases even suicidal impulses
can provide pleasure.

Again it is, as Bleuler contends, the will to reality which is the
earlier, not the will to hallucinate, as Freud believes. But to begin
with the contrast is nonexistent insofar as the individual feels
himself fused with the whole. We are so poorly oriented in that
reality which we later construct outside ourselves and confront-
ing us, that we are able quite ingenuously to employ highly fantastic means for the attainment of real goals. The schizophrenic,
on the other hand, lacks this ingenuousness, and reality in this
sense is not the *intention* of *his* autistic thinking.

Lastly, it is noteworthy not only how deeply our reality is
tinged by all sorts of autisms but also how it is based on thought
that is dominated by affects. In fact logical thought becomes feasi-
ble only by the cathexis of attention. Just as reality becomes

"real" only with aid of affects, so schizophrenic delusions are founded on some actual impressions. Nothing is born out of the nothingness, but the line is always a fluid one.

Bleuler holds that the schizophrenic is unhappy in his madness since his ecstasy is not persistent and his wish fulfillments do not satisfy him at all. Two further considerations must be added: first, schizophrenia is but the consequence of a failure to master life. Hence its delusions are just as exorbitant, as the resignation which enlisted their aid is terrible. Second, the schizophrenic does not envisage the attainment of his goals in *specific* wish fulfillments, but rather wishes himself to be the *whole*, to be All, as inadequately realized by him as is our need to be nothing but specific individuals.

Bleuler overlooks much of this because of his rationalism and an eye exclusively in search of the disorders of thought, as when he speaks of the unsatisfactory state of research on the intellectual aspects of autism. He puts autism between primitive reality function and logical thought, and he finds only in highly developed thought the synthesizing functions of fantasy which Freud considered most primitive of all, ascribing it even to the "hallucinating chick." The point, however, is not that reality function stands for the earlier behavior and hallucination for the later, but that we are ourselves able to imagine the earlier behavior only as physical or reflex activity, a purely preliminary stage, whereas it is in its own way all-comprehensive. As well as deny the autism of the chick we might say that only the chick in the egg exists where the schizophrenic longs to be—*in the totality*.

GÖTTINGEN, JULY 9-21, 1913

Rainer

One day there was Rainer standing at the garden gate in the twilight, and before we said a word we clasped each other's hands over the fence. The whole time that he spent here made me so very happy! Not just as a reunion, but because it was so very much a reunion with *him* who was other times so alienated and so deprived of reality by that "other one" (as we used to call it). To be sure I had always found him unmistakably himself in his letters, but now to find him day after day, in every mood, in every hour, even the worst of them, always himself: such a thing I could not recall from any other time.

The problem remained for us all the same, that in his heart and soul he did not feel better but actually worse than before. We talked a good deal about it. It is understandable that any improvement has to be paid for by this feeling of being worse. The very fact that he no longer comes apart into two beings, too alien from each other to suffer from each other, is enough to make him suffer from everything that is still not quite organized and realized in himself and yet is part of him and no longer a split-off personality. Simultaneously the distorted and aberrant elements in him seem now to make more for hysteria than ever before. The inner center of his personality no longer is split in two, but is maturing and growing in spite of everything. It remains his *body*'s task alone to express his difficulties. And not only paroxysmally as in the past or in isolated traits, but as a whole, his body now is much more disposed to illness; and it is a body that hardly ages, as though the maturity coming with years is substituted for by his sickly hesitation and inability to keep up with the real events of time.

Maybe it is for this reason that Rainer complains that while productive periods once they got under way in the past, would run their course without check, even taking over his body, now although his spirit is never enslaved as it used to be, neither is he ever undisturbed, so that characteristically his production has become fragmentary. Now he looks on his body itself as the "other."

There is a fearful danger here, danger of an augmented hostility to the body, and of a new introversion taking place just as the original one is at the point of yielding to his more complete psychic identification. In the prodigiously expansive way that he surrenders himself inwardly to things,—lyrically productive and hysterically sick—Rainer has always been alienated from the body, i.e., at pains to catch up with physical existence or find a substitute for it. But now this might culminate in a kind of hopelessness which is directed from the outset only toward spiritual substitution.

In his case the only index of these things is to be found in his creative work. With the following result: at the time he wrote the *Neue Gedichte* under Rodin's[91] influence, he took a sculptor's artisanship to be the same as the work of a lyric poet, and with most beneficial effect; he turned outward to things and his mind was relaxed. Now he looks on the work as a method, a road, a transition. On the other hand, the new technique in his most recent poems (*after* the *Marienlieder*) takes the opposite direction: to be sure, he wants once more to only express *things,* not himself reflected in his emotion, but doing so he turns his back on the very people to whom he addresses himself. (This is what he means by the selection of uninviting words.) Here I think there is no question of method in the sense of technique, which implies utterance and understanding; rather a new kind of introversion is taking place here as in the physical form mentioned above.

How mightily the *Elegies* soar above this, both in their promise and their fulfillment! As I read, comparing them with the very oldest "Christusvisionen" from the first year of our acquaintance in Munich, I was deeply struck by the pure and consistent line, from the earliest eloquent evocations of his innermost soul to the most recent ones. Long after his departure I sat thinking over these matters, and it was as though I wandered in a great garden where autumn was yet to come.

The breathing sphinxes.[92] Lotus-flower. Cow. Potter's wheel. Bedouin village. Bedouins with the brass draped in their lifted garment and the double shock of their pilgrim staff and their shouting. The Kaboul dog. *Toledo* as a hill among hills, the river running like a noose around its neck. The river on the way to Cordova, becoming light as it passed banks studded with somber mills and mirroring a blue house as though it were on holiday in its own blue color.

Greco's: *Assumption of Mary* almost thrust from below, drawn ever more gently ascending. The *Hour of the Cross*, actualized so to speak, as the drops of blood are caught by the angel, twisted almost horizontal in his haste, and by the angels on the side (extended wings; in the older pieces, the line of the nose and the sensuous line of the leg). *Toledo* with the hospital, too, on a cloud and rotated as well, not only removed from its place (there it would have blocked the view), the inscription below on the plain held by the Son. Greco in the Dresden gallery in October. *The Healing of the Blind*. The silence of the event (in secret like every miracle) in the midst of the groups in motion. Individuals on the alert, one who is gazing across. Self-portrait. Only the dog knew it all the time.

Duino garden: the wind below ever making its presence more evident and the clatter of footsteps on the stone stair, the mice and the thrushes imitating one another. Note: The productive mood is evanescent, its passing most easily expressed in horror—horror as of something real.

Dove hunting in the Duino (discussed when we were in the Riesengebirge, with the three dachshunds). When the aesthetic pleasure ran out, they replaced the doves by the dachshunds, the

familiar and beloved dachshunds. Rainer's protest: the possibility
of both delight and indignation side by side.

The bells of Chartres (chair and dizziness)—the goldfish. The
St. Sarah festival. Marthe. "Planchette." Нижинский.[93] Our frog.
Narcissus[94]

> This then: this emanates from me to free
> itself in air, the breath of forests, fleeing
> from me with ease, and casts away my being
> in splendor, safe from all hostility.
>
> Unceasingly this mounts above my soul,
> I do not want to leave, I linger waiting;
> but all my limits are in haste and grating
> have rushed away, and reached their goal.
>
> And even in my sleep. Too weak the tie.
> This yielding middle, kernel full of frailness,
> which does not hold its meats. Oh, how they fly
> from all my outer body's parts of paleness.
>
> What there is forming as I trust my own
> and trembles upward in a tearful turning,
> *that may perhaps in woman's womb have grown,*
> *her innermost; it was beyond my yearning,*
>
> *(however urgent was in her my try).*[95]
> Now openly it in the water cowers,
> in water unmoved and distraught, and I
> may wonder at it in my wreath of flowers.
>
> There it is unbeloved. Down at the dam
> of tumbled rocks' disdainful countenances,
> and I can see how sad, how sad I am.
> Was this the likeness mirrored in her glances?
>
> Did thus I leave to sweeter fear her breath,
> her dream? Almost I feel her own dejection.
> For as I lose myself in my reflection,
> I could believe that in my eye is death.

GÖTTINGEN, AUGUST 12, 1913

Lou Andreas-Salomé to Alfred Adler

I have waited a long time to write you, to formulate at least sketchily things I now see differently from last summer when I first wrote.

Do you recall what I said then: how, despite theoretical disagreement with Freud (which I then considered more essential than it turns out to have been), I still could go a long way with him without being bothered by it? Now it seems to me that that is intrinsic to the whole situation. It seems to me the whole theoretical disputation around Freud rests in a way on a misunderstanding which cannot be settled simply by comparing theories. To be sure my interests always lay there, and to begin with these things were only important to me in their philosophical context. But this is really about the most wonderful thing Freud has taught me: an ever renewed, ever deepened satisfaction in the facts themselves which he has discovered, and my satisfaction endures and forever puts me at a new beginning. For in his case it is never a question of finding out and assembling material details, which only would derive their true value from purely philosophical discussion. He has not unearthed ancient stones or implements; we ourselves are there in all the findings. Hence the insights put so plainly before us are no less philosophically important for us than are the child's experiences for him when he first learns to say "I."

If we submitted the outcome of Freud's research to a general formula and unified it in an abstract synthesis posed somewhat differently than before, it would not be decisively advanced or essentially altered. It would resemble those investigations of altruism, which correctly asserted that even altruism is only egoism. To be sure! But to investigate altruism one would have to create new subdivisions, analyze, and make distinctions. In such a way, something would remain in the net after fishing in the depths of the human soul which would make it possible to discover new empirical data despite the coarse mesh employed out of practical necessity for the purpose of unification.

Of course it is not at all your main purpose to include everything in a single formula (like the power instinct or "masculine protest"), but to base things on the concept of the feeling of inferiority with its organic foundation. Your first work approaching this idea from the physiological side was very important for me, and you already know how highly I appreciated the second one, coinciding with my work on the formation of religious fictions, and strongly corroborating it.

On psychoanalytic grounds, however, I have not been able to reconcile myself to an organic origin of inferiority feelings, and for this I have philosophical justification. In our eyes the organic as such neither explains nor determines the psychic. Rather it is its representation (and vice versa), and no matter how complete and authentic the representation seems to be, I could learn or deduce from it nothing at all about psychic processes, no more than I could the reverse. On the basis of its own methodology, psychology has the right to ignore this enigma, this obscurity, this X. Apart from any expression of epistemological opinion, psychology here proceeds in its own way, just as natural science goes on its own way uninfluenced.

If therefore it is not permissible to claim any priority for the psychic or the somatic, I cannot perceive how the psychic can be comprehended so negatively—as rising from a deficiency and preserved by fictitious devices. To be sure there does exist a struggle for power based on impotence, but only because we understand by the word "striving for power" or however else we may designate the thing at the moment, a synonym for life in general, permeating everything and everywhere, eternally the same. I am not persuaded that life, asserting itself to be sure in incessantly changing images, in fictions and symbols, is after all only an airy reflection in the void, a negation of a negation.

It was at tea at your hourse that first evening that I objected to this view, pleading with you in jest to oblige me by putting the concept "feminine" more positively. Even today, despite your arguments to the contrary, your "feminine means" is none other than the underlying drive which shows its claws in the "secondary safeguard" (and not just velvet claws but real ones masked as such). So I would take my stand just where I did at the start, beside Freud's Ucs. and beside the causal explanations which lead me to find his explorations in the depths (beneath all the things I have myself discovered to be true) more conclusive than all brooding about them.

VIENNA, AUGUST 16, 1913

Alfred Adler to Lou Andreas-Salomé

Do not think that I am thrown off base by criticism. But I would reproach you above all for being so unwary.

My position with respect to Freud's school has alas never had to reckon with its scientific arguments. All I ever see, all my friends ever see, is a busy-busy grabbing and pilfering and all the learned shenanigans of the kind Mach mentions in his *Analysis.*[96] Why is it that that school attempts to treat our views as common property, whereas we have always insisted on the errors of *their* opinions? But it is possible that—being unwary—you have observed nothing of this.

To me this is all proof that Freud's school does not believe in its own doctrines and really only wants to safeguard its investment.

There is a hitch in your analogy regarding altruism and egoism. I have maintained plainly enough that the nervous person has just that kind of sexuality and that degree of libido needed to rescue his feeling of individuality. And the same holds for his verbal modes of expression. It is irrelevant here that the two, libido and speech, have effects beyond the individual and even more irrelevant that they are composed of the material stuff that nature provides. They are not *natura naturans*, however, but constructs which the body creates as it presses to expand. That is how I can account for the libidinal transformations and even the teleological significance of the libido itself. But the expansive tendency can be accounted for on the basis of the libido only if the libido itself is assumed to have a yen for expansion.

That would be a logical error, if the Freudians had not committed it retrospectively in order to get around my contention. But this way it is no longer scientific at all.

Your second objection refers to the leap from physical nature to psyche. I do confess it is my secret conviction that I have had some success with it. Unhappily the others have not yet discovered it. *Psyche is a name for the life-potentiality of an inferior creature.* And it comprises the aggressive instinct, the tendency toward expansion, and a reaching out for that which is more highly valued culturally—the male.

One word about Freud's discoveries and explorations. Every single patient of mine makes discoveries of that sort. Which is not intended to be derogatory. It simply points out the fictions. Freud has taken *his* device for a reality. That is the crux of the matter. And now perforce he invents more fictions to cover up his deficiences. One question: do you really think people like us, if we had journals at our disposal, would carry on so merrily with fictions like "hushing-up tactics," "identification," and the rest? My opinions might be wrong! But is that a good enough reason to steal them too?

MUNICH, AUGUST 17-20, 1913

With Gebsattel: [97] *Art and Life*

At Gebsattel's before leaving for Vienna. Talked with him about Rainer starting with Rainer's portrayal of Нижинский which exists as a completed work of art inside him, not committed to writing only so that he can relive it over and over again through the spoken word. Thus alone a last impulse to do it remains alive (on the other hand, perhaps, because he is so often weary now and needs to turn to human company to get the impulse; hence his scintillating conversation and indeed his productivity—but to the point of exhaustion). It would be very interesting to know whether in such instances of needing to remain uncommitted we do not have art's confession of its incurable aloofness from life, at least romantic art as contrasted to classical, less pure and with a deeper longing for life.

On account of this aloofness it is never the creation of the work which is ultimately decisive; it is conceivable that productivity, in this sense a flagging one, when it at last comes to fruition does so the more profoundly as a sign of perfection. For Rainer's sake I wished this thought would become a ripened and attainable fruit, hanging ready to be grasped by his searching hand. (It is after all the problem of giving *form* which means at once to stand aloof and to give life.)

The fact that all art appears to be the result of repressed complexes as they become manifest conforms with art's aloofness from life when it reaches an exceptional degree of excellence. Art resolves these complexes through "social activity," achieving conscious form through expression.

Just as the complex does not thereby become conscious, so too aesthetic enjoyment advances beyond that instinctual stimulation which in the presence of a like content arouses action; the two remain "aloof"—the origin and the effect.

This is also the reason why any fortuitious bit of reality is segregated or "framed" for us (as when we gaze as it through a window or in a mirror) and why it seems as though we should try to lay hold of it by looking ever more closely at it and not by bringing its content into connection with the rest of the surrounding reality.

On Freud

Part of Gebsattel's critical attitude toward Freud stems from personal matters, as he imagines the personality of the man who came on these discoveries and interpreted them. My experience has been the exact opposite: for example, when I read the *Interpretation of Dreams* and realized what a self-exposure Freud had been forced to make at that time in the use of his data, and in the midst of a scornful and antagonistic crowd at that, I gained respect for the simple heroism of the man's life. To be sure the heroic and the all-too-human elements lie close together, especially for the psychoanalyst. But even aside from a purely scientific and unemotional evaluation of these discoveries, I consider respect more appropriate than personal criticism. Confronted by a human being who impresses us as great, should we not be moved rather than chilled by the knowledge that he might have attained his greatness only through his frailties?

VIENNA, END OF AUGUST 1913

On Narcissism

The arrival in Vienna was indescribably beautiful and so was the drive home, accompanied by Tausk, and my old hotel room, No. 28, with many flowerpots in the window. Even the employees gave me a hearty welcome. Something inexpressible about the hot depopulated town. (Every day strictly devoted to work.) During our work on narcissism Tausk made two observations: (1) "However insufficient determinism may appear in psychological matters, it is not so much because too many different determinants are at work as that they are disposed in such a variety of layers; this accounts for the opacity of the rest." (2) "It is essential to distinguish from narcissism the intellectual mechanisms that serve its needs."

In my opinion it is especially noteworthy that analytic practice touches on the limits of narcissism (taking Freud's definition of narcissism as a limiting concept) both in the infantile stage when there is no object and in the libido's vanity as it is directed toward the self as an object. But quite apart from that, narcissism accompanies all the strata of our experience, independently of them. In other words, it is not only an immature stage of life needing to be superseded, but also the ever-renewing companion of all life. Hence it is not merely the limit beyond which the analytic endeavor cannot prevail, but also the one in which the ego and libido interact to creative purpose. To that extent it is transpersonal, and hence for this quite positive reason it cannot be further dissected or made logical by empirical means.

I think Tausk also does not emphasize this point adequately in his definition of the libido, part of which (as Freud states it) stays with the ego and extends its grasp toward objects but is still able to withdraw it. While Tausk's explanation holds for artistic production and so on, it persists in regarding narcissism in the sense of a developmental stage, one which already having found an object still elects to return to itself. (This I consider most true in puberty when the new accession of centralized libido suffices to provide not only for the sexual instinct but also for the ego instinct, thereby uniting both in a narcissistic creative potency—in the mind as it does in the genital too under the stimulation of fantasies.) But, on the other hand, narcissism per se, underlying all the deeper activity of our life, persists still in "self"-forgetting identification with all that exists and hence in a rebirth of the ego in contrast to the contemplating, indulging self-centered attitude.

Victor Tausk

Tausk and I were arguing about the analogy of the alphabet. He said that if he were to be presented with the letters in a new and different order—as they might appear differently ordered to the beginner at learning the alphabet and reading words—he would undertake such an experiment. But it is inconceivable. He forgets that the analogy is valid only for logical formulation. The letters offer no new meaning to ideas that can be formulated. But just as they can have nothing but a supportive function themselves in the initial act of interpreting their meaning, so too with logically comprehensible ideas. The distortion of letter and meaning is transcended by the interpreter; likewise that between the individual, logical, and empirical datum and its interpretation within the context of human experience. Just as anything which is logically ordered requires a quantum of affect to gain our attention, so it is human experience alone that can subjectively solve the mystery inherent in objects. And human experience alone provides the sole objective bridge between individual analyzable facts and the meaning of the whole. It is not only the material for psychoanalytic investigation but also the coherence wherein all of reality abides. Being the umbilical cord which connects us to the whole, for all its essentially personal quality it is nonetheless the most objective thing, indeed the only objective thing, *constructing the object world not indirectly but out of itself.*

In psychoanalysis our thinking proceeds simultaneously toward two different goals. In resolving pathological ideas it endeavors to bring to consciousness elements that have become submerged into unconsciousness, and in so doing it stands on the laws of development. Conversely, in its approach to the deeper psychology of normal functioning, it discloses those other unconscious processes on which our conscious ego is itself grounded, and to this extent it is involved with the laws of being. In the second case however, where its most wonderful effects and discoveries may be found, it is imperative to take care lest practical analysis come to be forgotten for the sake of theoretical synthesis. Yet prudence can go too far even here.

Psychoanalytic thought can block synthetic thought instead of clarifying it if philosophical relations are not permitted to rest solely on their own merits—as they have every right—but get jammed once more by the very psychoanalytic media which helped to expose them. The psychoanalytic method of thinking holds to its own modes of thought within general psychology. Departing thence into the biological and physical realms it acquires a much more one-sided and a much more unequivocal precision; correspondingly it must grant free passage beyond its territory in the other direction—that of philosophy.

The danger is greatest in the case of those psychoanalysts who stand themselves in practical need of the method they profess. That is the only way I can understand how Tausk, endowed by nature with a philosophical head, has so to speak cut it off instead of using it, at least on holidays. When he engages in synthetic thought he promptly "thinks it over" with a bad conscience, since basically he always thinks of his *own* practical analysis alone—*never* synthetically; hence his position with regard to psychoanalysis is at once too uncritical and (through resistance) excessively critical. This is then laid at Freud's door.

Only now do I perceive the whole tragedy of Tausk's relation with Freud: that is, I realize now that he will always tackle the same problems, the same attempts at solution, that Freud is engaged in. This is no accident, but signifies his "making himself a son" as violently as he "hates the father for it." As if by a thought transference he will always be busy with the same thing as Freud, never taking one step aside to make room for himself. That *seemed* to depend so much on the situation, but ultimately it is his own doing.

It is quite plain that the additional difficult complications caused by his preparation for the *Rigorosum* (examination) and his domestic conflicts leave him no time to read, to orient himself in the publications pertinent to his problem. Still working with him, I feel clearly now that there are personal reasons for this also. What he *wants* is his blind and dumb self-expression alone, suffering so greatly as he does under the burden of himself.

Perhaps this too: a certain gap in creativity is filled by identification with the other (sonship) which constantly begets the illusion of having attained the anticipated position.

It is interesting and curious too how someone can come on the most profound discoveries in all his analyses,—all of them being displacements of his own, his longing for discovery being only the longing to be analyzed himself—and yet pass right by things in front of him if they happen to involve himself. When I told him of his own maternal being he was at first like one set free; then the next days he was in a greater torment than ordinarily. The measure of resistance that had blocked this insight needed to find an outlet somewhere. Were it not for the pathological development, how wonderful would this motherliness be in him, elaborated from inversion into tenderness and ardor of the understanding and combined with the great energy that often seems so naïvely healthy. How exceptionally beautiful that would be. At moments when he behaves that way he reveals distinctive gestures which seem so peculiar to Tausk and which give promise of something in him that he *is not* (maybe something that was or will be, maybe something that no longer has any substance). And then there still remain those irreconcilable contradictions between that which Freud calls the "beast of prey" (which at least helps him in the practical management of life) and his oversensitivity to the point of self-dissolution.

It is all so painful to behold that one would like to look the other way and run away. He is deceiving himself about me with his fantasies. In the long run no helpful relationship is possible; there can be none when reality is cluttered by the wraiths of un-abreacted primal reminiscences. An impure tone resonates through everything, buzzing as it were with murmurings from within.

Yet from the very beginning I realized it was this very strug-gle in Tausk that most deeply moved me—the struggle of the human creature. Brother-animal. You.

SEPTEMBER 7-8, 1913

Munich Congress

On coming from Vienna on September 6, and arriving at the Bayerische Hof, I met Freud before going with Rainer to Geb-sattel's. Spent the evening with Freud, Abraham,[98] *et al.* in the lobby.

At the congress the Zürich members sat at their own table opposite Freud's. Their behavior toward Freud can be charac-terized in a word: it is not so much that Jung diverges from Freud, as that he does it in such a way as if he had taken it on himself to rescue Freud and his cause *by* these divergences. If Freud takes up the lance to defend himself, it is misconstrued to mean that he cannot show scientific tolerance, is dogmatic, and so forth. One glance at the two of them tells which is the more dogmatic, the more in love with power. Two years ago Jung's booming laughter gave voice to a kind of robust gaiety and exu-berant vitality, but now his earnestness is composed of pure ag-gression, ambition, and intellectual brutality. I have never felt so close to Freud as here; not only on account of this break with his "son" Jung, whom he had loved and for whom he had practically transferred his cause to Zürich, but on account of the manner of the break—as though Freud had caused it by his narrow-minded obstinacy. Freud was the same as ever, but it was only with difficulty that he restrained his deep emotion; and there was nowhere I would have preferred to sit than right by his side. Tausk consequently also sat very close by, despite the fact that Freud plainly held him off now, although he himself admitted that in this new situation Tausk was the right man ("clever and dangerous," said Freud, "he can bark and bite"). Now at last all political maneuvering was at an end after a winter when it reigned supreme; one could, one ought, one had the right to thunder. And Tausk knew how. He had to leave again on the second morning, after he had done his task. But Jung had improperly shortened the time for our paper. Gebsattel and I left with him and I continued on to the train, thus missing Bjerre's paper[99]—inadvertently. (He had oddly selected that short case in Helsingfors, which we certainly did not look on then in *that* way. This time however his views won the support of the Zürich people.) Gebsattel heard the paper. He wandered around among the parties indifferently, with his cigarette between his lips, as if it were a deliberate impediment to keep him from commenting or breaking into laughter. He sat down at last in Freud's corner however, as I was bringing Rainer. I was delighted to bring Rainer to Freud, they liked each other, and we stayed together that evening until late at night.

The day after the congress, September 9, with Freud in the Hofgarten. The long conversation (in confidence) on those rare instances of thought transference which certainly torment him. This is a point which he hopes need never again be touched in his lifetime; I hope the contrary. In a recent case the situation goes like this: one problem involves affects, that the woman had to speak with such emotion after so many years about a fortune-telling which was *not* fulfilled as if it had been fulfilled. It was simply because (as was revealed in psychoanalysis) it all had come true in her mother's life, hence as if her mother's life had already modified hers too, while she consciously suffered from her own frustrations. The second problem involved the manner of the transference to the fortuneteller. He reads off to her and expresses in realized form not only her conscious wishes but also those that lie deep behind her consciousness. It is hard to say where there would be any bottom to these depths.

Thirdly, there is a question of timeless duration within us. Freud always emphasizes that by "timeless" he means unabreacted and no more. But that does not explain many things; even the fantasies of dementia, which Jung described and which bring to life the mythology of primal antiquity, are themselves like enduring primal wishes and images in the abundance with which they are repeatedly brought to life and in their primitive nature. And in the case at hand the mother had indeed abreacted that which had retained its intensity in the daughter, quite as though it were her own, far beyond her own experience.

Here we approach the psychologistic boundary. It is very perilous, for Freud must guard particularly against being confused with the mystagogues. Here a philosophic attitude is no more to be evaded; we do live through more than we are.

SEPTEMBER 10-11, 1913

With Ferenczi

Worked with Ferenczi who stayed a while longer in Munich for that purpose, starting early, partly at our place (Gebsattel) and partly at his. His findings disturb him for reasons quite opposite Tausk's: being of philosophic (synthesizing) nature they do not get in the way of Freud's, but just because of their nature they are not looked on very kindly by Freud (who recently wrote in his daily notes "once again spent the evening 'philosophizing,' naturally seduced thereto by Ferenczi"). Ferenczi suffered as a child from insufficient recognition of his accomplishments, and it interfered with his diligence. Now alongside his publications, these works of his that contain his innermost spiritual experiences run a rather secret course because they are unappreciated. It is interesting how even in the midst of his work he himself tries to run away from them, although he is passionately determined to pursue them.

Our conceptions are so fundamentally in opposition to one another that they come near to making contact once more. Everything that Ferenczi calls "death tendency" from his point of view could also be called "life tendency" without thereby altering anything other than the purely personal outlook. Whatever might be imagined to exist behind the only forms of life we know can be conceived of as the "essence of life," quite as well as "absolute rest," whence only the first "impulse to motion" would be unknown. It is all nothing but words and intimations, which merely express the values we put on our life. Ferenczi, who would like among other things to interpret many biological facts from the side of the psyche (just as hitherto the reverse process has usually predominated), by and large once again adopts the physical explanatory model of the world: equilibrium, ultimate rest as the goal, and so on (although, even in the natural sciences, views on this point are in a state of uncertainty, considering that all these propositions are valid only for a closed system of space). This tendency was already made clear in Ferenczi's article on "Stages in the Development of the Sense of Reality":[100] proceeding from the original condition of the infant in the womb as the pleasurable condition of peace devoid of wishes, which the needs of life transform into one of unwilled living activity (fully in conformity with Freud's concept). But it must be remarked here that in this *identity* with the womb, a pleasurable condition of rest devoid of wishes is absolutely inseparable from the activity of the womb; both form a single reality in which no condition of enjoyment or of wishing could develop because of this complete living activity, while later when we are confronted by an external world such conditions develop within us. The manifestation of that which we call "soul" presupposes such a distance; when the distance becomes especially great and our inner unity is disturbed, we long for absolute peace, as the removal of the disturbance rather than allow that vital *identity to go on pulsing within us through every articulation of the inner and the outer worlds*. I cannot escape the idea that the tendency to death and rest—which Freud attributes to every living being as its essential being, inborn, and from which it is reluctant to be disturbed—is itself a rather neurotic estimation of life. The exactly opposite construction claims the same privilege: everything that has been organized and thrust into the course of existence is a piece of the original vital impetus which brings it to realization and out of which it constantly arises.

It is almost amusing how these two possible positions intersect in respect to sexuality; there alone reigns the tendency to return to the undifferentiated identity and to death through love. But precisely there arises the unforeseen result of multiplication, fertility, life. Whence the paradox comes that preachers of death are generally antisexual and preach abstinence, and so they discharge the persecuted drive and the desire, which only wanted to. die of itself. For practical purposes, however, Freud comes to other conclusions which serve life's purposes: every failure of adaptation to reality is for him the great defect, for we cannot expunge anything from reality, we remain locked within it, and only knowledge can make us at once calm (actually meaning resigned) and thereby relatively gratified.

Note: The oscillation between the death tendency and the need to live bears the mark of unity or, in the speed of the oscillation, the mark of the persistent becoming of unity.

SEPTEMBER 17, 1913

The Occult

Evening with Prof. Staudenmaier from Freising, whom Ferenczi also visited last year. While he was with us (i.e., at Gebsattel's) we suddenly discovered that he is not an investigator of artificially produced states of possession but is himself insane. Imperceptible change in everyone's behavior except Gebsattel's (although he was the first to change the subject of inquiry to new matters of interest). He won Staudenmaier's heart by his (gentleman's?) circumspection.

With regard to the matter of occult tales with which Rainer is momentarily occupied and which also come to us through Rega Ullmann,[101] Gebsattel's comment last summer is strikingly correct: facts thus communicated become worthless for scientific research since even if they came pouring down to us from worlds of miracle they needs must be accommodated to criteria valid for our inner and outer perceptions if they are not to be falsified right off as data. Quite a different matter from dreams and delusions where we know the mechanism behind which their exact content may be concealed.

On the other hand the psychology of mediums who are neither insane nor dishonest remains a problem which I should like to tackle with Ferenczi.

The way that in spiritualism different persons manifest themselves as one recalls Fechner's[102] fantasies of the demons that enter different people with different parts of themselves so that it requires a gathering of several to produce a "demonic center."

SEPTEMBER 29-30, 1913

Max Scheler[103]

When Gebsattel and I arrived at his (Scheler's) place in Tegernsee our initial conversation was very lively. He maintained the principle of solidarity in nature, in the sense that the tendency to fight is to be considered a deficiency and a transition of the milieu, so individualized that they not only do not disturb but actually advance one another.

His reduction of everything to love and hate seemingly puts him close to Freud, but only seemingly. ("The ancient loves and hates of our ancestors are all that we ourselves observe.") He considers them as final "data" [104] (in his phenomenological use of the word) apart from any developmental factors. He said very well: "Constants are always data without progress, only something lower 'develops.' " With this I could heartily concur. But he holds as objective that which is already in contact in the individual in constant and infantile form; here on the other hand Freud does not emphasize enough the significance of the primary creative life of man which he now calls "narcissism"—where despite all development we remain ever at home.

His distinction from Simmel's[105] logicism may be that Simmel only condescends, as it were, to attribute epistemological value to immediate experiences along with the logical, whereas for Scheler the quest for logical criteria of truth is already a sign that one does not yet "have" the essential element of it. "To have" means "to stand at the center of it and hence also to represent in personal terms" not "by virtue of self-contemplation," or "feeling as if" but "in the thick of it."

Gebsattel and I met with Scheler twice by appointment in the English Garden.

He spoke the other day, almost like Adler, of reason as the calculating principle which draws its substance from scarcity, from organic insecurity. But he comprehends in a most un-Adlerian way the source of all positive values in *abundance*, a view with which I am in sympathy. Also in economic terms: needs basically originate from that which was once luxury, superfluity. (I should prefer the idea that luxury once again be based on religion, like the sacrificial meal consumed in the company of God, and so on. A sort of recollection of universal ownership, only transformed to private property and so to comparisons, which for the neurotic becomes of *first* importance since he only goes back some stages of the process but not to the primary foundation equally close to every point.)

Last time he had fine things to say about the Greek theory of motion, a theory of discontinuity so to speak, mechanized by us later: man as stone, there almost stone as man. The fullness of mechanization has recently approximated the Greek view, insofar as the something in motion is reduced by physics to the point that it is no longer comprehensible in physical terms (practically made metaphysical in Scheler's view?). Roux[106] who previously emphasized the separateness of the component parts of the organism now emphasizes the self-regulatory mechanisms.

Here dematerialization means vitalization, life excludes inertia.

Scheler said smiling of old age in this connection: to the degree that the capacities wane, the spirit becomes active and in process. (But he then became disquieted about "his old age.")

And with all the interrupted leaps and bounds in his brilliant conversation—often following one another disconnectedly—the most enduring impression is really this: a tremendously logical mode of expression grounded in tremendously personal experience. But while he departs here too from Simmel, it is this personal element in him which is so peculiarly evident in his thinking; helping itself so to speak out of a personal conflict, it almost reaches the proportions of a reaction formation. The interruptions, the leaps, seem to betray a continuity in their psychic foundations. One actually can follow him with the greatest speed and assurance if one has initially recognized this, following it unswervingly through the complexities of the content. Scheler's *seriousness* is only thus rightly to be appreciated, and yet his humor too is qualified by it: when he laughs in mid-thought he is like a child caught in the act, caught by himself perhaps in the act of using his thinking as a means to his own inner unification (and consciously—for unconsciously we all do it). This is what he is *looking* for; he does not have the (Semitic) intent on the impossible, but since he is only in *search* of unity and does not possess it within himself his optimism is often brave indeed, but a little shallow. The subjective fullness harbored therein exists at the expense of objective profundity—at least that is so on occasion. His philosophy acquires its allure from its transparency as a form of self-analysis and self-healing, but that is also what makes it fragile. His concept of value—its keystone, from all I hear of it appears to me rather like a wooden sword, like something at once metaphysical and empirical and wanting to be neither. His evaluations of "data" always presuppose the mind that registers them (and Scheler himself spoke laughingly of what would become of phenomenology if tailors' minds publicly announced their data). On the other hand an objective character is supposed to be comprehended by his philosophy as merely a pale reflection of Platonic ideas. To dissolve them (the evaluations) to subjectivity would undermine the very ground which sustains Scheler's optimism and on which he makes his escape. But he fears to dissolve the subjective element *within* them—if not metaphysically then mystically, undividedly—because he wants to assert himself as an individual through and through and not surrender himself (lack of assurance in his own unity). On modesty. On suffering as purge.

Scheler made the good observation that in Freud's school one too frequently gives ontological priority to the simplest and least valuable thing, whereas it might simply be only the most banal thing, the best preserved.

Gebsattel and Scheler reciprocally reproach each other with their ethics. Since Gebsattel takes his stand on the either-or decision, he looks to Scheler like the Junker officer for whom *action* is everything, even when he thinks. Gebsattel says with greater justice of Scheler that he never escapes from *values* despite his wish only to "contemplate" without prejudice. Hence, his "data" continue to mean this or that to him, persisting in isolation and hence, whether he likes it or not, always humanly and to that extent rationally, discriminated. Whence intellectualism as a reaction against intellectualism. Since his recent departures, these fixed demarcations have become more fluid, but it will only amount to a raging sea of grain, a sea of sand.

How fine is the little analysis of Kant (in *Formalism in Ethics and the Ethic of Material Value*)[107] according to which Kant's formalism arises from mistrust in what is given by nature. But how close to that would be a self-analysis which would interpret Scheler's philosophy also as a reactive symptom.

Postscript on Max Scheler

Love and hate, in the sense of phenomenological "datum" instead of being explained—as Freud explains its *becoming*, and particularly that of sexual development. It is a start perhaps, but to be so it would have to give up all claim to being a part to geniune scientific research, because there is still a remnant which can be worked out further only experientially, never by Scheler's route which is actually a blushing metaphysic. In any immediate act of being, his evaluating cannot be expressed phenomenologically but only mystically, or rather it is inexpressible *because* it is mystical.

What is for *him* the indispensable element in his orientation is especially perspicuous in the fine book *Feelings of Sympathy*.[108] He enumerates there three kinds of sympathy—and of these he considers that the first (mere emotional contagion) has been erroneously taken as the basis for all theories of compassion: (1) sympathy with that which another person has to suffer for himself; (2) sympathy as one's own suffering apart from the fact of his; (3) finally sympathy as the highest form of love uniting the other two in itself. All three are ultimately based on a unity of being without which neither contagion nor understanding would be possible. Yet there is in fact a fellow-feeling, a compassion, that does not develop into contagion from this general basis but instead lifts it to consciousness from unconscious (and hence affectively helpless) existence. Whence new experiences of oneness with one's fellow-men are disclosed, common experiences of joy as well as of suffering (which is the sort of thing the metaphysicians of India, Schopenhauer, and others also had in mind without realizing it). Scheler does not think of these things because in love as in compassion he wants to remain the "one" continuing beside the "other," unmerged, and yet he looks for salvation in exaggerating the value of love and so on, thus compensating for this loss. But the finest new values of life might be attained in the growing awareness of the eternally present unity which, apart from the character of the individual affective organization, affords new loyalty and warmth (already immanent in narcissism).

BEGINNING OF OCTOBER 1913
Rainer and His Mother

Rainer's dream of his mother, in which he calls her "cocoon." An empty chrysalis—while he has the silk thread by virtue of his genius: that is the way I imagine their connection. In her mother, his grandmother, great vitality with an inclination toward pure, nearly childish hedonism. In her, this tendency almost paralyzed by her dreary marriage that provided her with no love at all and brought her hysteria to fruition. Now no more enjoyment of life: spiritually, however, the same tendency to self-indulgence, empty exaltation, fancy phrases. She is always hollow in her relations with *another* person, never meeting him, never reliable in practical things, but honest in mood and pleasure. This expansiveness is bound to Rainer's lyric gift by a delicate emphasis, maybe for that very reason such a horror to him, not just annoying like his father's philistinism. He acquired from that just a dash of pedantry which he handles like a balance pole; so as to keep sight of certainty and order amidst the greatest uncertainty. There is health in that. It is significant that his mother possesses none of this: she is able to sit comfortably in her ancient decrepit rooms in Prague, rooms abounding in memories, and complain—if only her own immediate person and grooming are in order—that she lacks Rainer's almost incredible involvement with his inanimate environment (which he brings to life), although for him it is only another substitute for security, for he considers all these fine arrangements and accords to be within himself.

When I recently came to know Phia in Munich personally, I was struck however by a physical resemblance: the Slavic element, in her case in its dark aspects, the soft parts of the face. His glance becomes ominous and indignant while she in her womanly way merely holds forth with inane emphasis. It poisons his unrestrained facility in conversation, which often replaces his ability to produce, and for which in a higher sense his fellow-man serves only as a means of release. Hence he gladly excuses my frightful indolence when in society, and when I apologized for it he said "most holy conception of Mary."

Rainer and I are going on a trip in the mountains via Dresden.

DRESDEN AND HELLERAU, OCTOBER 5-7, 1913

Rainer and Werfel

Rainer and I have met Werfel[109] here. Rainer has been experiencing Werfel ever since his departure from Göttingen. I read his handwritten copies of Werfel's first poems from *Wir Sind*. It was lovely and moving to see him experience this: feeling longing and joy, and free of envy, just as one comes to know his "son" as his "heir." The essence of it was the impression of shining naïveté with which Werfel seems to have bypassed all Rainer's dark conflicts—as one happy in the possession of all his memories; the sound of it rose clearly from the unbroken energy of his verse. Only two things might perhaps be disconcerting: his being so well read when so young, and (I thought) his exclusively humanitarian bent, i.e., suffering everything from the human point of view and taking everything emotionally (most beautifully in the "Damenkapelle"). I only grasped it in our personal acquaintance, when it became clear in his intelligent (very intelligent), and totally sincere conversation to what an extent poetry is for him a means of rescue and release from want and contradiction—the very antithesis of naïve effusion. In Werfel's own words its function is to exhibit—quite different from Rainer's case (for whom it is all a release into himself and not a form of human communication). Poetry in contrast to faith. Substitute for faith. The birth of the extremely positive out of negation and deficiency, the spirit out of polemic. When Werfel recited his poems (including the new and very beautiful one, "Der alte Lehrer") his total sincerity was most attractive—no trace of reaching for effect; but Rainer found his emphases conventional. All in all, they gazed at each other in astonishment, and despite the honest vigor and the great intelligence of this precocious being, the meeting did not result in the expected sonship: "I cannot embrace him!" Rainer said sadly.

OCTOBER 10-16, 1913

Rainer in the Riesengebirge

Rainer's ambivalent attitude toward his father underwent an unequivocal religious transformation after the latter's death: no longer the irrational source of disturbance—now he was as it were the invisible bringer of blessings in whom one found rest and refuge (his father's death itself left him rather cool at the time, perhaps in anticipation of this but also perhaps in a speedy mental repudiation of its horror. I remember how he avoided traveling from Berlin to Prague to see the dying man still alive).

When the old ebony walking stick he had inherited broke last summer—the silver handle of which his father held at the little boy's eye level in all their walks, Rainer shuddered and was shocked, as though it were the ominous destruction of something which had grown to be an organic part of him, something which infused him with the power of his father.

It is one of Rainer's most appealing qualities that despite his delicacy, on account of which anything violent threatens to subjugate him, such subjugation nevertheless does not lure him to effeminacy but breaks him down instead. It is on account of this definitely masculine element in him that one must avoid anything that might oppress him and use one's own powers lightly in order to give him his freedom to create.

At Krummhübel on October 11, we consulted Dr. Ziegelroth (director of the sanitorium), but Rainer naturally was unable to speak openly with him. His hemorrhages appear to be of no consequence. It does seem consequential to me that these congestions are located in the rectal as well as the nasal regions and have definitely undergone sexual displacement upward, as they formerly were displaced downward. (MARGINAL NOTE: gazing instinct —self-surveying—in shaving—embracing "with the eyes" as the only means of gratification and repose. Hence too the significance of the bisexual meaning of the eye.) The whole rectal region persistently sensitive, whereas genital sensations are so readily disposed to disgust; on the other hand exaggerated importance of everything connected with speech and tone. It is his mouth that has been most strikingly altered in the past decade, with the protrusion of the lips, and his big eyes stand out above with infinite sorrow.

Rainer's bisexuality is sufficiently developed for the feminine element to impair his full enjoyment of normal sexual intercourse: such appears to be the case at present. On the other hand, neither can his masculinity attain full satisfaction, since its most complete expression lies in production and takes a rather contemptuous view of this enjoyment. But his recourse to self-gratification (with normal heterosexual fantasies) once again aggravates his essentially noxious hostility to the body, and his introvertedness. And for this reason: the body becomes in one's own judgment thoroughly contemptible to the extent that emphasis is put on the organ itself; only the *reality* of another person has the power to make it a spiritual experience through symbolization. One thus misses not so much the person as the spirit.

We discussed Freud's remark: our ancestors celebrated the instinct but we legitimize it by means of the object. To Rainer and me that romanticism is embarrassing when it is actually a substitute for the originally profound, almost religious conception of the instinct itself.

The idea of the "phallic hymns" that persists in Rainer's mind is a superb one. At any rate he attempts thus to exalt that which comes to fruition too little in erotic object attachment; as always, here too poetry is his means of self-transfiguration.

During our return journey from the mountains we engaged in a dream analysis in the course of which many remote recollections of childhood stood out in Rainer's memory.

The washerwoman in the family household, who appeared to him to be the most important and powerful person partly because of her great massive body, partly because she was summoned only for hard jobs requiring physical power. She apparently haunted the little boy in his dreams with a mixture of horror and rapture.

At all events, a feeling since his early erections as of a living thing, part of himself, but also as a power outside him: something too great, too gigantic, only with an effort maintained as a part of him and experienced painfully, painfully in his need to pulsate through and with it. Malte Brigge's expression: "pulsating through two hearts." [110] This had a fearfully augmented effect during fever, yet he could not put his anxious ideas into words or give any details about them. Anxieties associated with old prohibitions of masturbation by his father seem to play a part, his father having cautioned him about where to put his hands when in bed. That is the point of a second terrifying fantasy: of being thrown out on a stone floor, touching it with his back and, especially, his neck. Sometimes in association with an image of a tomb, not enclosing him but close beside him, so that the elevated gravestone being inadequately supported might fall down beside him and graze him (thus he lay as it were between visions of the grave—death and something menacingly alive which he could not master and make his own, just as he could not save himself from death or escape it.)

The "desire for unrequited love" found as early as in Malte Brigge, acts contrary to his glorification of *woman's* capacity for love, like a temptation "to be loved like that." But the woman in Rainer feels corrupted by it, identifies with it, and so lives its life fully. By this circuitous route the man in him is seduced by the woman in him—not by the external woman—whence the conflicts arise. Hence too, they are unavoidable nor is there any escape from introversion. A final basis: the infantile desire to be loved, which becomes lyrical oneness with the world.

Rainer's Dreams

On the trip from the Riesengebirge to Dresden, October 16. He comes as though a spectator on a place where the grass is faded and trampled, closed in by cages holding large animals. But the real action in which he was not just a spectator took place earlier, and was speedily quite forgotten; it too concerned animals in cages and among them a snake seems to have appeared. Now when he approaches, walks over to the place, he sees only a lion: *très pâle*, which signifies: "remembered," "mirrored," or "blanched" (all this occurred to him in French words in the dream). The cages are of wood quite freshly painted green (occasioned by the *Oktoberwiese*).[111] In the center a naked man (sketch of a nude by Cézanne); over the pallor of the nude violet shadows appearing in the dream as "complementary colors" to the green of the cages. Diffuse light. The man is standing in the posture of a waiting model put on exhibit with the animals, not of an animal tamer; his limbs in repose.

Rainer's earlier dream at Göttingen in July. He steps up to a mirror and first thinks he sees himself in the reflection till he recognizes it is his father: grown smaller than he, a little bent and sad, holding his head to one side. This dream accompanied by a strong affect of horror and melancholy.

"The mirror," "mirroring," as earliest childhood impression; from that time when dressed as a girl (Renée) he stood in front of it; often rushing through all the rooms to look at the mirror, whenever he had been disguised in some costume, or ornaments, or a mask.

"The mirror" in the fragments of the elegies: as if ultimate things there were rising toward creative release. At this point I therefore broke off the other dream analysis (third dream?), as though there would be an encroachment on that which needed to remain in darkness. *Il ne faut plus approfondir ça.*

(MARGINAL NOTE [written in Rainer's own handwriting]): Toward the end of the dream I found myself in a kind of a hospital or hospice lying in bed beside other beds; it was clear that I possessed the appropriate documents giving me the right to be in this institution, yet there was something about my reception that was in dispute, not quite in order. A man, a sort of overseer, appeared, who I immediately assumed would turn to me to investigate this point, which he indeed did. He came to my bed and I had time to notice that he wore an old uniform which I found particularly repellent in that it had a high (red) collar of the meanest sort, twisted and with a filthy border. It was an impression that had been always among the most painful in my experience. (In postmen, porters, musicians.) When at last he stood before my bed and I looked up at him he surprised me by another much more unusual quality. That is, his eyes were empty, and one could see through them into the inside of his very round head, right into an inner space bounded posteriously by a second inner forehead. This quite new phenomenon made me very wary and preoccupied with the "empty room" in his head. Then I awakened.

Associations: Mirror—Bed.

It is as though the corpse of the man next to him were being bathed. As though it were his father's. Uncanny. And yet a relief in contrast to what preceeded, which had been forgotten. Especially clear, the opening of the door and the passage of the overseer through the room.

Recollection from childhood; uncertain whether a daydream: a room with a stove, behind it a gaping hole through which it is possible to see into the darkness, the hole of exactly the same proportions as the stove standing upright next to it.

This recalls the empty orbits with the second forehead behind and especially the old childhood nightmare of the gravestone next to the open grave beside which Rainer sees himself lying.

DRESDEN, OCTOBER 17-21, 1913

Sexuality

Just as our participation in everything, our identity with everything persists and surrounds the ego consciousness we have so firmly established, so similarly within the realm of the ego there abides that which we call "voluptuousness." While it feels like something of a special and more specific quality, in reality it envelops the entirety of life within us and around us. The wonderful vitality and fullness of life, mysteriously binding us to the universe, permeates our being without being pressed into consciousness so that in romantic language and in the enthusiasm of sensuality, of transcendent sensuality, it is called "spiritual," simply because it would be an even narrower construction to call it "physical."

Hence in love we misunderstand each other even more in the realm of sense than in that of the spirit, for we can express ourselves with far greater immediacy in spiritual terms than there where we first have to translate ourselves into consciousness *even for ourselves*. And the tragedy of it too is that it is not so easy to recognize our misunderstanding there as in the spiritual realm, since the more typical means of expression is deceptive.

If we think of the primitive phallic cult we perceive how fully the phallus represented something divine, comprehending the person and the world, and took symbolic form by means of sex, even though—no, *because*—it represented unconditioned reality itself. The material component was thus as much the basis of existence as it was its *mysterium;* so too, sexuality could signify the basis of naked existence and at the same time God. This was known to all ancient art: not only does the spiritual manifest itself materially in the work of art (which was of course at the same time the work of religion) but matter itself is a symbol. That alone is the reason why an Egyptian cow of even the tiniest dimensions breathes "eternity" and why all realistic art however technically perfect is profane and inferior, and differs from high art in more than degree (as Worringer[112] shows so well).

Hence the phallus, naked, dumb, physically inarticulate, holding all of being latently within, could tower up as obelisk. Only for us has it come to be something half to titter at, half to shudder at, equally remote from worship as from common sense, something in which the immature child in his horror suspects the contradiction between appearance and meaning and which for the adult becomes triviality or hysteria.

Among other things it is this that lends significance to sexuality: that it can go so much further to comprehend pain than can the self-assertive drive of the ego. By the very fact that it dissolves our ego boundaries, pain is no longer only destructive but under certain circumstances may be a source of sensual pleasure. Happiness can only stay with us a short time without turning through excess into pain and overwhelming us. Hence it is most essential to experience beyond the narrow confines of the ego that happiness which is related to all things spiritual because it has already transcended its own personal limits, and while indeed happiness has thus become nameless.

Generally we break up everything piecemeal into sorrows and joys, and it is only in our highest moments that we know how in the background life streams in its most vital course when we no longer ask whether it flows bitter or sweet. In psychoanalysis we discover the pathological causes of depression, but in many cases those of gladness also. Perhaps it would be correct to say that the heaviest laden of men, in perfect health, would react in such a way that insofar as his sufferings were irrevocable he would go out of himself as a part of the world—a world he himself now represents and which constitutes his own reality (like the world of the blind, the despised, the hated, and so on). In certain crises of disease, and just before certain agonies, a person is often no longer the subject but a third person; this kind of splitting furnishes a fine antithesis to pathological splitting—for to be *entirely* one with the self means to be able even to abandon the self.

We experience fully only when we are joined in union with our experience, as if our subjective awareness and the external reality were twin beings. Whatever befalls us happens only partly to us; for the rest, we are ourselves the event which consciousness artificially separates from us and opposes to us. Beyond all the assertions of our consciousness there is need of a *faith* for full experience, and only in that faith lies a genuine grasp of reality.

Man and Woman—Bisexuality

Since sexuality is physically and mentally more stressed in woman than in man it has long been customary to identify universal human qualities with *masculine qualities*. But one must not forget that when not behaving in the characteristic way of his sex—i.e., aggressively, but culturally, or with kindness, or with intellect—the male necessarily employs his passive and hence female aspect. And while woman on account of her passive sexual orientation discovers something unsexual as it were in all the domain of the ego, the intellect, and culture and is able to include it in her femaleness, the male is erotically injured thereby; for him it denotes domestication and the enfeeblement of his purely aggressive element.

In Freud's terminology, the civilization of the male would mean an elaboration of homosexuality. Certainly it is only those slightly homosexual men who see the universally human qualities in woman and are erotically disposed toward them. (MARGINAL NOTE: Except for artists, who need their bisexuality all for themselves.) Men with no homosexual tendency whatever remain even in their most powerful and most genuine passion inclined toward the purely female—plus friendship and the like, excluding erotic rapture.

The firmest union of masculinity and femininity is comprised by motherliness, where woman conceives and bears and also generates, protects, and governs the offspring. So it is with the man when he rules and decides, but as a knight in service, i.e., on behalf of the beloved person.

The masculine component in woman, the feminine in man, that everyone possesses, operates differently in individual cases, with respect to the effect of bisexuality on the whole person. It emancipates the one from his own sex, creates a disturbance of harmony, defeminizes the stamp of womanhood, effeminizes the man. Others on the contrary are only the more deeply tinged in the spiritual hue of their sex, as the bisexuality stands out in contrast to a less empty and colorless background of sexuality. It is as if one were oriented by the constant presence of a partner within making for a higher unity of one's own, which for that reason can never become a fully realized one-sidedness. Only in this situation can bisexuality become fruitful, and here the creative type is separated by a very sharp line from the merely complacent, even in the case of the unproductive man, i.e., the man who only produces himself.

BERLIN, OCTOBER 22-29, 1913

Resistance—Repression

Hours with Eitingon.[113] He too said in conversation about the Munich Congress: the best thing now would be for the whole association to blow up; in that way like minds could find one another honestly, and Freud would not be forced to go to war against attacks from his own camp or to protect those who stand with him without being able to give full guarantee for their correctness (e.g., inferior supporters).

In the psychoanalytic session, which was mightily lacking in spirit, I got interested in Eitingon's paper although it did not provide anyone with a problem for discussion. In his "meagre" case which plainly he presented for just that reason, the question should have been raised where the principal distinction lies between "lack of talent" (meaning the failure of the unconscious to be made manifest) and "resistance," for both of them can only represent degrees of repression up to the point where the repressed seems to have become the *natural* basis on which the total personality is built. To that extent a fluid line would be possible between neurosis and psychosis.

Abraham merely contributed a comparison with a manic-depressive patient; this comparison however poses quite another problem, since we do not understand how the broad range of the manic-depressive could be attained in that condition despite the steady and stupid unproductiveness of the unconscious.

Furthermore the question concerning resistance or individual function is interesting not only from the side of the pathological but from that of the normal. In fact, all our actions and our being are accompanied by the resistance of repression. Its failure, the lack of inhibition, would mean illness and destruction. Just as it is part and parcel of the psychic rhythm, so it belongs to the most primitive physiological structures, since the irritability of the simplest bundle of protoplasm is manifested by ingestion and defense and only thus proves itself to be alive. Freud little by little—not in the early writings—recognized the repressing force as a concomitant of organic development, i.e., not *only* as a cultural factor or one produced by outer influences or pathologically. Still, the line between normal and pathological repression is a shifting one. And I cannot escape the doubt whether too much has been attributed to the account of the pathological. For example I do not find it convincing that the infantile amnesia is entirely a product of repression; it is more than likely that we forget what we have experienced through the medium of the feebly developed intellect so that it is on the one hand more un-differentiated and on the other too isolated in its detailed content. Freud of course does not assume that this amnesia is pathological, but he does assume it to be determined by the presence of experiences of pleasure which had to be suppressed. The question may very well be asked whether the mistake does not lie here: because infantile "sexuality" itself had been posited too definitely (as if his own sharp terminology had duped him) "repression" has the same fate.

One of the difficulties consequent to this is the assumption of the persistent contrast between man's psychic mechanism and his instinctual life, even though Freud makes it comprehensible by means of the ego instinct. In Jung's hands it becomes purely a mystery how libido turns against itself and is transformed into culture and, so to speak, devours itself in the living body. Considered philosophically, this deflection into the desensualized cultural sphere can be found in Freud's theory too because of the antithetical tendencies of the unconscious and consciousness through which repression attains its fatal triumph in the sequence of sublimation. Yet Freud's view with the clear separation of *pathological* and *natural* repression, as between the life-inhibiting and the life-forming, does not give rise to this theorizing pessimism.

GÖTTINGEN, BEGINNING OF NOVEMBER 1913

God

In the God-father concept, the self and the other once more form an unbroken unity for the believer out of which we just emerge at birth—for we do not come out of duality but only

enter it in our conscious existence. Perhaps in that way the father did not gradually become God, but the divine totality still
glowed around the father who represented it, as our immediate
environment. One might at heart believe that it is on account of
the force of conscious experience alone, the dualistic cleavage into
human existence, into ego and world, that God was somehow for
primitive man the first and only certainty; God was, so to speak,
his recollection.

In the fundamental condition that accompanies us all our lives
(and especially penetrates all creative experience) where we with
redoubled strength feel ourselves to be ourselves and yet at the
same time identical with all, megalomania *and* absolute dependence seem to flow into one another; and the piety of all times
and all men has been so characterized. Once, when words were
first being formed and before they were fixed by usage, any one
word could easily express the divine (and many a word which we
now consider as fetishistic and coarsely religious did only that),
but when all words became fixed, they thrust out the divine into
the neighboring region of superstition.

Unlike many others I do not believe that primitive man lacked
a sense of causality or an inclination to reality: I rather believe
that is where man *began*. But this was overcome by the tendency
of that act of fantasy which preserved the lost unity in the god.

Conclusion

The way in which one beholds a person in psychoanalysis is
something that goes beyond all affect toward him; somewhere in
the depths both aversion and love become only differences of degree.

A relationship is achieved beyond one's own fidelity or infidelity.

Approximately this way: if hitherto one had so swiftly and so forcefully penetrated the partner that he too soon and to one's own disappointment was left behind, one now would turn quietly, strangely, and see him following and be close to him. And yet not close to him, but to all. Close anew to all, and in it, to oneself. And all the vanished persons of the past arise anew, whom one has sinned against by letting them go; they are there as from all eternity, marked by eternity—peaceful, monumental, and one with being itself, as the rock figures of Abu Simbel are one with the Egyptian rock and yet, in the form of men, sit enthroned over the water and the landscape.

Notes

1. "Vom Frühen Gottesdienst," *Imago*, II (1913), 456-467.
2. *Lebensrückblick*, (Zürich: Max Niehans Verlag, 1951).
3. *Lebensrückblick* (Zürich: Max Niehans Verlag, 1951), p. 16.
4. Personal communication.
5. E. F. Podach, *Nietzsche's Zusammenbruch* (Heidelberg: Niels Kampmann Verlag, 1931).
6. "Gedanken über das Liebesproblem," *Neue Deutsche Rundschau*, XI (1900), 1009-1027.
7. Quoted by Ernst Pfeiffer, ed., *In der Schule bei Freud* (Zürich: Max Niehans Verlag, 1958), p. 232.
8. "Jesus der Jude," *Neue Deutsche Rundschau*, VII (1896), 342-351.
9. Rainer Maria Rilke and Lou Andreas-Salomé, *Briefwechsel* (Zürich: Max Niehans Verlag, 1952).
10. Herman Nunberg and Ernst Federn, eds., *Minutes of the Vienna Psychoanalytic Society* (New York: International Universities Press, 1962), Vol. I. "1906-1908."
11. Ludwig Binswanger, *Erinnerungen an Sigmund Freud* (Bern: Francke Verlag, 1956), p. 62.
12. *Mein Dank an Freud* (Vienna: Internationaler Psychoanalytischer Verlag, 1931).
13. Ernest Jones, *Life and Work of Sigmund Freud* (3 vols.; New York: Basic Books, 1953), Vol. III, p. 453.
14. See note 11.

15. Sigmund Freud and Oskar Pfister, *Psychoanalysis and Faith,* tr. Eric Mosbacher (New York: Basic Books, 1963).

16. Ernest Jones, *Life and Work of Sigmund Freud* (3 vols.; New York: Basic Books, 1953), Vol. III, p. 204.

17. H. F. Peters, *My Sister, My Spouse* (New York: W. W. Norton, 1962), p. 288.

18. The correspondence has not yet been published in full. See Ernest Jones, *Life and Work of Sigmund Freud* (3 vols.; New York: Basic Books, 1953), Vol. III, Appendix A, for several of these letters from Freud to Lou Andreas–Salomé.

19. See note 1.

20. "Zum Typus Weib," *Imago,* III (1914), 1-14.

21. "Der Mensch als Weib," *Neue Deutsche Rundschau,* X (1899), 225-243.

22. " 'Anal' und 'Sexual,' " *Imago,* IV (1916), 249-273.

23. Sigmund Freud, *Three Essays on the Theory of Sexuality* [1905], tr. James Strachey, *S.E.* (London: Hogarth, 1953), Vol. VII, pp. 125-245; (New York: Basic Books, 1963).

24. "Narzismus als Doppelrichtung," *Imago,* VII (1921), 361-386; English translation by Stanley A. Leavy, *Psychoanalytic Quarterly,* XXXI (1962), 1-30.

25. See note 12.

26. Sigmund Freud, *Gesammelte Werke* (London: Imago, 1950), Vol. XVI, p. 270.

27. Lou Andreas–Salomé, *Mein Dank on Freud* (Vienna: Internationaler Psychoanalytischer Verlag, 1931), p. 72.

28. The Third Psychoanalytic Congress, September 21-23, 1911. Lou Andreas–Salomé attended it in the company of Dr. Poul Bjerre, whom she had been visiting in Stockholm.

29. Ellen Delp was a younger friend of Lou Andreas–Salomé, whom she met earlier in the year in Berlin in association with a group of Max Reinhardt's actor-friends

30. Ludwig Jekels (1867-1954) was then a physician in Vienna who had joined the Psychoanalytic Society in 1909.

31. Wilhelm Stekel (1868-1940) was one of the four original members of the Psychoanalytic Society; he founded the *Zentralblatt für Psychoanalyse* with Alfred Adler in 1911. In the winter of 1912, Freud

resigned from the editorship of that journal and soon thereafter began the *Internationale Zeitschrift für (ärztliche) Psychoanalyse*.

32. Hermann Swoboda (b. 1873) had been a Dozent in Psychology at the University of Vienna. He is mentioned by Freud in *The Interpretation of Dreams* as "a youthful philosopher," who "has undertaken the task of extending to psychical events the discovery of a biological periodicity (in twenty-three-day and twenty-eight-day periods) made by Wilhelm Fliess." Sigmund Freud, *The Interpretation of Dreams*, tr. James Strachey, *S.E.* (London: Hogarth Press, 1953), Vol. IV, p. 94; (New York: Basic Books, 1959), p. 94.

33. Along with Stekel, Alfred Adler (1870-1937), a Viennese neurologist, joined Freud's group in 1902. He became chairman of the society in 1910. His departures from Freud's views are to be observed in their process of development in the *Minutes of the Vienna Psychoanalytic Society* (see note 10). His observations and theories have been presented in a selection from his works by Heinz and Rowena Ansbacher in *The Individual Psychology of Alfred Adler* (New York: Basic Books, 1956), a volume which has been consulted for use of Adler's terminology in English translation.

34. Alfred Adler, *Uber den nervösen Charakte; The Neurotic Constitution* (New York: Moffat, Yard, 1916).

35. *Imago* was a psychoanalytic journal which began to publish in 1912. It was largely devoted to literary and philosophical applications of psychoanalysis.

36. Victor Tausk (1878-1919) was originally a prominent lawyer in Bosnia, who later gave up this profession on account of personal difficulties and became a journalist in Berlin and later in Vienna, where he studied medicine. He belonged to the Vienna Psychoanalytic Society from 1909 until his death by suicide in 1919. He is best known for his paper "On the Origin of the 'Influencing Machine' in Schizophrenia," English translation by D. Feigenbaum, *Psychoanalytic Quarterly*, II (1933), 519-556.

37. Martin Buber (b. 1878), the Jewish philosopher and theologian, had been the editor of a series of sociological writings, and it was at his request that Lou Andreas–Salomé wrote her short book *Die Erotik* (Frankfurt am Main: Rutten & Loening, 1910).

38. Paul Federn (1871-1950), a Viennese physician, was an early fol-

lower of Freud. He practiced psychoanalysis from 1903 until his death in New York in 1950. He was president of the Vienna Psychoanalytic Society from 1924 until its dissolution by the Nazi government in 1938. Many of his papers are to be found in Paul Federn and Edoardo Weiss, eds., *Ego Psychology and the Psychoses* (New York: Basic Books, 1952).

39. *Studie über die Minderwertigkeit von Organen* (Berlin and Vienna: Urban & Schwarzenberg, 1907). *Study of Organ Inferiority and Its Psychical Compensation: A Contribution to Clinical Medicine* (New York: Nervous and Mental Diseases Publishing Company, 1917).

40. Carl Gustav Jung (1870-1961) introduced psychoanalytic methods and concepts in Switzerland soon after the publication of *The Interpretation of Dreams* in 1900. He became personally acquainted with Freud in February 1907, the year of the publication of his important early work, *The Psychology of Dementia Praecox* (English translation by A. A. Brill and Frederick Peterson ["Nervous and Mental Disease Monograph Series," No. 3.], New York, 1909). He was elected president of the International Psychoanalytic Association at its founding in 1910 in Nürnberg. His first serious departures from psychoanalytic thought appeared in 1911 and 1912, especially in his *Wandlungen und Symbole der Libido* (Leipzig: Deuticke, 1912); "Symbols of Transformation," *Collected Works* (New York: Bollingen Foundation, 1956), Vol. V.

41. Isidor Sadger was a neurologist in Vienna who adhered to the Psychoanalytic Society as early as 1906. He wrote pathographies of C. F. Meyer, Nicolaus von Lenau, and Heinrich von Kleist and at length on sexual perversions. The lectures referred to in this journal appear to constitute the work published in 1913 in the *Jahrbuch der Psychoanalyse* under the title "Über den sadomasochistischen Komplex," Vol. V, pp. 157-232.

42-43. H. Oppenheim and Carl Furtmüller were early adherents of Adler's dissident group.

44. See note 40.

45. Maximilian Harden (1861-1927) was a publicist, editor of the weekly *Die Zukunft*, in which some of Lou Andreas-Salomé's essays were published.

46. Otto Rank (1884-1939) was a favorite pupil of Freud's and, from 1906 to 1915, the official secretary of the Psychoanalytic Society.

His important works—*Der Mythus von der Geburt des Helden*, *The Myth of the Birth of the Hero* (Vienna: Deuticke, 1909), ("Nervous and Mental Diseases Monograph Series," No. 18. New York: Nervous and Mental Diseases Publishing Company, 1914), and *Das Inzest-Motiv in Dichtung und Sage*, *The Incest Motive in Poetry and Saga* (Leipzig and Vienna: Deuticke, 1912)—had already been published. His differences with Freud appeared much later and became evident in his book, *Das Trauma der Geburt* (Vienna: Internationale Psychoanalytische Verlag, 1924); *The Trauma of Birth* (New York: Harcourt, Brace, 1929).

47.
> *Alles Vergängliche*
> *Ist nur ein Gleichnis.*
>   (Goethe *Faust* II. final chorus)

48. Sándor Ferenczi, a Budapest neurologist engaged in psychoanalysis from 1908, proposed at the meeting in Nürnberg in 1910 the formulation of an international association. He accompanied Freud and Jung on their journey to America in 1909 and was on close personal terms with Freud for many years. For the bulk of his writings see *Selected Papers of Sándor Ferenczi* (3 vols.; New York: Basic Books, 1950-1955).

49. Gaston Rosenstein was a Viennese analyst who on this occasion had delivered an address on "Periodicity in Dreams." See note 32.

50. This fantastic form of treatment may have originated in the theories of Wilhelm Fliess (see note 53), but found no favor in psychoanalysis.

51. The meeting with Jung in Munich is described in a letter from Freud to Ludwig Binswanger published in the latter's *Erinnerungen an Sigmund Freud* (Bern: Francke Verlag, 1956), p. 62, n. 50. Freud wrote in this letter of November 28, 1912, of the complete reconciliation of the differences between him and Jung.

52. On the Macduff legend, see Sigmund Freud, "Contributions to the Psychology of Love: a Special type of Object-Choice in Men" [1910] *S.E.* (London: Hogarth, 1957), Vol. XI, p. 173. *Collected Papers of Sigmund Freud* (5 vols.; New York: Basic Books, 1959), Vol. IV, p. 201.

53. Wilhelm Fliess (1858-1928), Freud's friend and correspondent during the years 1887 to 1902, was a nose and throat specialist in Berlin, sympathetic at first toward Freud's revolutionary ideas. He

is of special importance in the history of psychoanalysis since he was Freud's sole confidant as to ideas and troubles at the beginning of his psychoanalytic career. His major interests were in periodicity and bisexuality. Freud's letters to Fliess have been published with an introduction by Ernst Kris, *The Origins of Psychoanalysis* (New York: Basic Books, 1954).

54. Otto Weininger, in 1902, published a book called *Sex and Character* (New York: Putnam, 1914), in which he made use of Fliess's theory of constitutional bisexuality, having learned of Fliess from Swoboda, who in turn had consulted Freud because of a neurosis. A controversy over priority between Fliess and the two "rediscoverers" ensued. See *The Origins of Psychoanalysis* (New York: Basic Books, 1954).

55. Eduard Hitschmann (1871-1958) began the practice of psychoanalysis in 1905. In 1911 he published *Freud's Theories of the Neuroses* ("Nervous and Mental Diseases Monograph Series," No. 17. New York: Moffat, Yard, 1917). He was later director of the psychoanalytic clinic in Vienna. His last years were spent in the United States.

56. Goethe remarked to Eckermann about Serbian poetry in translation on January 18, 1825: "The poems are magnificent. Some of them surpass the 'Song of Songs,' and that is saying something."

57. Alfred Freiherr von Winterstein became a member of the Vienna Society in 1910. The paper referred to here, "Psychoanalytische Anmerkungen zur Geschichte der Philosophie," was published in *Imago*, II (1913), 175-237.

58. Poul Bjerre was a physician specializing in Stockholm in the practice of psychotherapy. Lou Andreas–Salomé met him there while on a visit to the famous feminist Ellen Key.

59. Victor-Emil Freiherr von Gebsattel (b. 1885) met Lou Andreas–Salomé at the Weimar Congress. An adherent of psychoanalysis at this time, he later became known best as a writer in the field of phenomenological psychiatry.

60. Richard Beer–Hofmann (1866-1945) was a Viennese poet whom Lou Andreas–Salomé met in 1895.

61. From "Notes upon a Case of Obsessional Neurosis" [1909], *S.E.* (London: Hogarth, 1955), Vol. X, p. 248; *Collected Papers of Sigmund Freud* (5 vols.; New York: Basic Books, 1959), Vol. III, p. 383.

62. Leonard Seif was a Munich physician who first belonged to the psychoanalytic group in Zürich and later established a group in Munich.

63. The telegrams announced the death of Lou Andreas–Salomé's mother in St. Petersburg.

64. This was the third of the studies included in *Totem and Taboo* [1912-1913], *S.E.* (London: Hogarth, 1955), Vol. X, p. 75; (New York: Moffat, Yard, 1918).

65. See *S.E.* (London: Hogarth, 1958), Vol. XII, p. 303, *Collected Papers of Sigmund Freud* (5 vols.; New York: Basic Books, 1959), Vol. II, pp. 144-147.

66. Emil Franz Lorenz was a physician from Klagenfurt, who was invited to speak to the Vienna group. His paper, "Die Geschichte des Bergmann's von Falun," was published in *Imago*, III (1914), 250-301.

67. Rudolph Reitler (1865-1917) was a physician in Vienna who was a member of Freud's group from 1902 on. Freud characterized him as one of the most important pioneers in the movement. His writings dealt principally with symbolism.

68. This little poem, here freely translated, comes from Goethe's letter of July 17, 1777 to Auguste zu Stolberg. See J. W. Goethe, *Gesamte Ausgabe* (Munich: Deutscher Taschenbuch Verlag, 1961), Vol. III, p. 268.

69. James Jackson Putnam, Professor of Neurology at Harvard, was won over to psychoanalysis by Freud's lectures at Clark University in 1909. He attended the Weimar Congress and was a founder of the American Psychoanalytic Association. It was his interest in relating psychoanalysis to philosophical and ethical values that stimulated the sharp debate of which Tausk's discussion was part.

70. Marie von Ebner-Eschenbach (1830-1916), Viennese novelist, became acquainted with Lou Andreas–Salomé on the latter's earlier visit to Vienna in 1895.

71. Gertrud Eysoldt, actress.

72. Karl Weiss was a physician in Vienna. This paper was published in *Imago*, II (1913), 552-572.

73. Presumably the allusion is to the fourth section of *Totem and Taboo* (see note 64) in which Freud discussed the significance of the primal parricide.

74. See Introduction, page 19.

75. Helene Stöcker was an old Berlin acquaintance of Lou Andreas–Salomé, at this time a member of the Berlin psychoanalytic group which was principally concerned with social reform.

76. Theodor Reik, one of the few nonmedical psychoanalysts in the Vienna group, had written a paper on the great writer of short stories and novels, Arthur Schnitzler, which appeared in *Imago*, II (1913), 319-335.

77. Herbert Silberer, a physician in Vienna, joined the Vienna group in 1910. He was the author of many studies of mysticism, symbolism, and magic. His best-known contribution concerning the "functional phenomenon" in dreaming was discussed by Freud in *The Interpretation of Dreams*, S.E. (London: Hogarth), Vol. V, pp. 503f.; (New York: Basic Books, 1959), pp. 503-505.

78. S.E. (London: Hogarth, 1959), Vol. IX, p. 117; *The Collected Papers of Sigmund Freud* (5 vols.; New York: Basic Books, 1959), Vol. II, pp. 25-26.

79. "The Claims of Psychoanalysis to Scientific Interest," *S.E.* (London: Hogarth, 1962), Vol. III, pp. 165–190.

80. *S.E.* (London: Hogarth, 1953), Vol. VII, p. 161.

81. Friedrich Schiller: *Das verschleierte Bild von Sais*.

82. *Hans Vaihinger, The philosophy of "As If,"* English translation, 1926.

> The expression was coined by Hans Vaihinger and applied to his own system of philosophy, according to which all human knowledge, all explanations in the realm of science, philosophy, law, religion, etc., are merely so many fictions or assumptions which tell us that the things or events, etc., referred to are or behave "as if" they had such or such a character, or "as if" they had been produced in such and such a way.
>
> *Encyclopedia Brittanica*, Vol. II, p. 544.

83. Hanns Sachs, a lay analyst, founded the periodical *Imago* in 1912. He had been a member of Freud's group since 1910. He lived later in America.

84. Presumably Dr. Poul Bjerre, according to H. F. Peters. *My Sister, My Spouse* (New York: W. W. Norton, 1962), p. 272.

85. This was probably an anecdote told by Gustav von Salomé (1804-1879), the father of the writer, who had been a general in the Rus-

sian army. The Decabrist revolt of the Russian officer nobility took place on December 14, 1825 (old calendar), and was suppressed by Tsar Nicholas I. See Sergei Pushkarev, *The Emergence of Modern Russia, 1801-1917*, translation by Robert McNeal and Tova Yedlin (New York: Holt, Rinehart, & Winston, 1963), p. 69.

86. *S.E.* (London: Hogarth, 1958), Vol. XII; *Collected Papers of Sigmund Freud* (5 vols.; New York: Basic Books, 1959), Vol. IV, pp. 13-21.

87. "The Antithetical Sense of Primal Words" [1910], *S.E.* (London: Hogarth, 1958), Vol. XII; *Collected Papers of Sigmund Freud* (5 vols.; New York: Basic Books, 1959), Vol. IV, pp. 184-191.

88. Sabina Spielrein was a Berlin psychoanalyst. The reference is to her paper, "Destruction as the Cause of Becoming," *Jahrbuch der Psychoanalyse*, IV (1912), 465-503.

89. Carl G. Jung, "Wandlungen und Symbole der Libido," *Jahrbuch für psychoanalytische und psychopathologische Forschungen*, III-IV (1912); English translation by Dr. Beatrice M. Hinkle, *Psychology of the Unconscious* (New York: Moffat, Yard, 1917). The critique by Ferenczi is in *Internationale Zeitschrift für Psychoanalyse*, I (1913), 391-403.

90. Eugen Bleuler (1857-1939), Professor of Psychiatry at the University of Zürich and Director of the cantonal mental hospital, Burghölzli. The reference is to his paper, "Die Psychoanalyse Freud's, Verteidigung und kritische Bemerkungen," *Jahrbuch für psychoanalytische und psychopathologische Forschungen*, II (1910), 623-730.

91. Auguste Rodin (1840-1917), the French sculptor. Rilke acted as his secretary from 1905 to 1906.

92. These are notations by Lou Andreas-Salomé of incidents narrated to her by Rilke during his visit. The events took place in the interval of his travels after 1909 in Algiers, Tunis, Egypt, Spain, Duino Castle, France, Dresden, Göttingen. "The potter's wheel," see in the ninth Duino Elegy the line "pots by the Nile." "The Kaboul dog" is referred to in a letter by Rilke to Lou Andreas-Salomé, written March 16, 1912: "In Kairouan, south of Tunis, a yellow Kaboul dog jumped at me and bit me." For "dove-hunting in the Duino," see Rilke's comment on the eleventh sonnet of the second part of the Sonnets to Orpheus: ". . . in certain chalky

regions the . . . doves of the grottoes are frightened out of their subterranean shelter by waving the cloths that have deliberately been hung in their holes, in order to kill them when they fly out in terror." "The St. Sarah festival," a Gypsy festival in Provence; "Marthe," a girl in Paris. "Planchette"—while in Duino on 1912, Rilke participated in attempts at automatic writing. "Our frog" was in the park at Göttingen.

93. Vaslav Nijinsky, the great Russian dancer.

94. This poem, here translated by Albert Ehrenzweig, was originally published as a note to Lou Andreas-Salomé's essay, "Narzismus als Doppelrichtung" (see note 24). (It is not included in the English translation of this paper.) This part of her essay concludes as follows:

> It is somewhat to the discredit of the godfather of our term, Narcissus, hero of the mirror, if its use brings to the fore only the erotism of self-enjoyment. Bear in mind that the Narcissus of the legend gazed, not at a man-made mirror, but at the mirror of Nature. Perhaps it was not just himself that he beheld in the mirror, but himself as if he were still All: would he not otherwise have fled from the image, instead of lingering before it? And does not melancholy dwell next to enchantment upon his face? Only the poet can make a whole picture of the unity of joy and sorrow, departure from self and absorption in self, devotion and self-assertion.

The original poem is as follows:

> Dies also: dies geht von mir aus und löst
> sich in der Luft und im Gefühl der Haine,
> entweicht mir leicht und wird nicht mehr das Meine
> und glänzt, weil es auf keine Feindschaft stösst.
>
> Dies hebt sich unaufhörlich von mir fort,
> ich will nicht weg, ich warte, ich verweile;
> doch alle meine Grenzen haben Eile,
> stürzen hinaus und sind schon dort.
>
> Und selbst im Schlaf. Nichts bindet uns genug.
> Nachgiebige Mitte in mir, Kern voll Schwäche,
> der nicht sein Fruchtfleisch anhält. Flucht, o Flug
> von allen Stellen meiner Oberfläche.

Was sich dort bildet und mir sicher gleicht
und aufwärts zittert in verweinten Zeichen,
das mochte so in einer Frau vielleicht
innen entstehen; es war nicht zu erreichen,

(*wie ich danach auch drängend in sie rang*).
Jetzt liegt es offen in dem theilnamslosen
zerstreuten Wasser, und ich darf es lang
anstaunen unter meinem Kranz von Rosen.

Dort ist es nicht geliebt. Dort unten drin
ist nichts als Gleichmuth überstürzter Steine,
und ich kann sehen, wie ich traurig bin.
War dies das Bild in ihrem Augenscheine?

Hob es sich so in ihrem Traum herbei
zu süsser Furcht? Fast fühl ich schon die ihre;
denn wie ich mich an meinen Blick verliere,
ich könnte denken, dass ich tödlich sei.

95. The italics are Lou Andreas–Salomé's.

96. Ernst Mach (1839-1916), the philosopher. The reference is to *Die Analyse der Empfindungen und das Verhaltnis des Psychischen zum Psychischen* [1897], English translation by C. M. Williams, *Contributions to the Analysis of Sensations* (Chicago: Open Court, 1914).

97. See note 59.

98. Karl Abraham, psychoanalyst in Berlin, president of the International Psychoanalytic Association in 1924. He was much admired by Freud and wrote many of the still fundamental papers on psychoanalysis.

99. Poul Bjerre, "Bewusstsein contra Unbewusstsein," *Jahrbuch fur psychoanalytische und psychopathologische Forschungen*, V (1913), 687-704.

100. Sándor Ferenczi, "Stages in the Development of the Sense of Reality," translated by Ernest Jones, *Sex in Psychoanalysis* (New York: R. Brunner, 1950).

101. Rega Ullmann was a poet and a friend of Rilke.

102. Gustav Theodor Fechner (1801-1887) first stated the concepts of psychophysics, which influenced Freud's theories of dreaming and

of the relationships obtaining between stimuli and sensations. Following a severe mental illness Fechner wrote books of an animistic-theological nature, probably referred to here.

103. Max Scheler (1874-1938) was a philosopher of phenomenology, engaged in studying the essential nature of mental attitudes and their objects and differing from his teacher Edmund Husserl in independently according real status to the objects. In philosophical psychology his book *Wesen und Formen der Sympathie* (1923), has been translated into English by P. Heath, *The Nature of Sympathy* (New Haven: Yale University Press, 1954).

104. "Data" in German, *Gegebenheiten.*

105. Georg Simmel (1858-1914), philosopher and sociologist, was a friend of Lou Andreas–Salomé for many years.

106. Wilhelm Roux was the Director of the Anatomical Institute at the University of Halle. He presented the concepts of functional adaptation and self-regulation in 1881.

107. *Der Formalismus in der Ethik und die materiale Wertethik* (Halle: 1913-1916).

108. See note 103.

109. Franz Werfel (1890-1945), poet and novelist.

110. The reference is to Rilke, *Die Aufzeichnungen des Malte Laurids Brigge* (Leipzig: Insel, 1910).

111. *Oktoberwiese* is a country fair.

112. Wilhelm Worringer analyzed artistic style as an expression of a period or nation. His work on Gothic style, *Formprobleme der Gothik* (Munich: R. Piper, 1927); (London: Hogarth, 1930).

113. Max Eitingon became acquainted with Freud's work while still a student in Zürich. He also was later a president of the International Psychoanalytic Association.

Index

Abraham, Karl, 14, 168, 190

Abu Simbel, Egypt, 21, 193

Adler, Alfred, 2, 13-14, 18, 51, 84, 87, 174; address to Medical Society, 44-45; "circle" of, 42-43; critique of, 126-128; first visit to, 34-35; Freud and, 62, 88, 132, 158; on homosexuality, 52-54; inferiority theory, 129; letters from, 33, 35, 160-161; letter to, 158-160; on nature of neurosis, 37-38; organ concept of, 110-111; on somatic foundation of neuroses, 54-55

affection, 119

alcohol, homosexuality and, 76-77; masturbation and, 76

ambivalence, 98, 127, 147-148; love and, 137

anal erotism, 17, 23, 57, 59

"Anality and Sexuality" (Andreas-Salomé), 23

analyst, versus analysand, 72-74

Andreas, Friedrich Carl, 7, 9, 21

Andreas-Salomé, Lou, Adler and, 126-128, 158-160 (see also Adler, Alfred); on anal erotism, 17, 23, 57, 59; analytic studies written by, 22-23; autobiography of, 7, 24-25; biographic details, 3-8; Freud and, 3, 10, 20-22, 25, 37-40 (see also Freud, Sigmund); Göttingen period, 21-22; last years and death, 25-26; on narcissism, 15-17, 24 (see also narcissism); on religion,

26; Rilke and, 10-11, 154-157, 178-185 (see also Rilke, Rainer Maria)

anxiety, 116; enchantment and, 149; hate as, 94; pain and, 141

archaic thought, 151

art, as repressed complexes, 162

autistic thought, 152-154

Bachofen, Johann Jakob, 114

baroque, 120-121

Beer-Hofmann, Richard, 8, 19, 76, 91, 99

Binswanger, Ludwig, 13, 20

bisexuality, 87, 99-100, 188-189

Bjerre, Poul, 71-72, 137-140, 169

Bleuler, Eugen, 127, 152-154

Bonaparte, Napoleon, 139

body–mind interaction, 55

Buber, Martin, 8, 37

cat, narcissistic, 88-89

censorship, concept of, 86-87

ceremonial, phobia and, 112-113

child, lies told by, 79-80; self-control in, 92

childhood sexuality, 90-91

childhood traumas, 91-92

cognition, 145

commonplace, life and, 117

compassion, 143

complexes, concept of, 39; repressed, 162

compulsion neurosis, 112-114

countertransference, 72